MAKING ROCKING HORSES

KING-HORSE

Anthony Dew

MAKING ROCKING HORSES

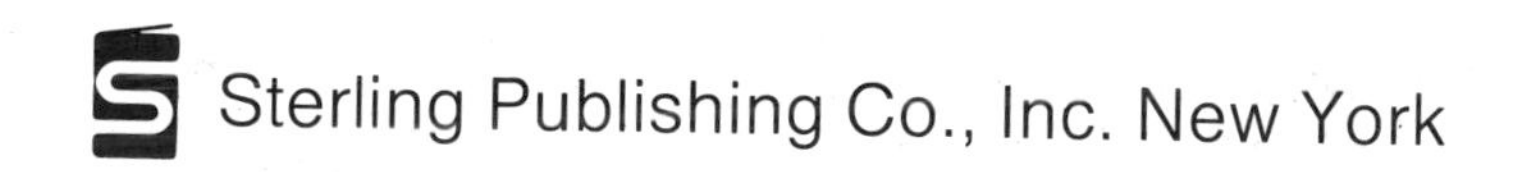
Sterling Publishing Co., Inc. New York

**To Pat and our children,
Sam, Kate and Lynn**

Frontispiece The large rocking-horse, with its three-year-old rider

Published in 1984 by
Sterling Publishing Co., Inc.
Two Park Avenue
New York, N.Y. 10016

Library of Congress Cataloguing in Publication Data

Dew, Anthony
Making rocking horses.

Includes index.
1. Wooden toy making. 2. Rocking-horses. I. Title.
TT174.5.W6D48 1984 745.592 84–2694
ISBN 0-8069–5528–7
ISBN 0-8069–7916–X (pbk.)

Printed in Great Britain

Published by arrangement with David & Charles Ltd.
This edition available in the United States, Canada and the Philippine Islands only.

CONTENTS

Foreword 7

1 **Why a Rocking-horse?** 9
Hobby-horses — Pull-along Horses — Early Rocking-horses — Fully Carved Rocking-horses — Renovating Old Rocking-horses

2 **Two Hobby-horses** 19
The Plywood Hobby-horse — The Solid Head Hobby-horse

3 **The Simple Rocking-horse** 29
The Rocker Base — The 'Mark 1' Cut-out Head — The 'Mark 2' Simple Carved Head — The 'Mark 3' Carved Head

4 **The Traditional Fully Carved Rocking-horse** 45
How to Tackle Carving — Types of Timber — Making the Horse — Stands and Rockers

5 **Renovating Old Rocking-horses** 104
Woodworm — Broken Ears and Jaw — Loose or Broken Legs — Paintwork — The Stand — Tack and Finishing

Appendices
1 Conversion Table for Scale Drawings 117
2 Gesso 118
3 Suppliers of Tools, Accessories and Fittings 121

Glossary 123

Acknowledgements 126
Index 127

MADE IN ENGLAND
10 × 14

FOREWORD

Since becoming a professional 'rocking-horse man' I have found, to my surprise and delight, no end of fellow enthusiasts. In spite of the plethora of electronic games and space age playthings this simple toy remains a faithful source of pleasure for children (and, of course, parents and grandparents).

As a child I always liked making things, but became seriously involved with woodworking only later — I suppose because when I was at school manual skills were rather looked down upon. I abandoned an early career at sea to become a woodworker, but it proved harder than I thought. Desperate for work of any kind, I took a job as a building labourer. It was a 'one man' building company and the boss reluctantly agreed to try me out for a couple of weeks. After two days he told me I was 'a dead loss as a labourer', and then flabbergasted me by asking, 'Do you think you could hang doors

Plate 1 (opposite) The author working on a large head

Plate 2 No rocking-horse is so badly damaged as to be irreparable!

and fix a skirting board?' That day I began to learn the trade of joinery.

Eventually I took a college course, in which I specialised in wood sculpture and carving. Part of the course involved a project which had to take the form of something you might be commissioned to make. I wanted to carve something fairly big, because I like hacking away at a sizeable chunk of timber with my mallet and gouge. I also wanted it to be something to do with children — a rocking-horse was the obvious choice. I like any kind of woodcarving, but I like it most if it does something.

That first rocking-horse helped me pass the college course and then for years it was passed round various relations until it came back to us after the birth of our first baby. It was big, over six feet long, and what an ugly thing it was! Having made or renovated hundreds of rocking-horses in the intervening time, my ideas about rocking-horses had moved on a long way. I became embarrassed about having it in the house and finally took it anonymously to an auction house and got rid of it. It's the only rocking-horse I have ever really disliked, but I hope nevertheless it is giving pleasure to someone right now.

Since I started making rocking-horses the products of my chisel have been in a continual process of change and, I hope, improvement. They have certainly moved much more towards the traditional style of rocking-horse than those I made at first, though I treat each horse as an individual and no two are the same. I have even been asked to make a rocking unicorn — but I will never make a rocking spaceship.

Apart from making new rocking-horses from scratch, renovating and restoring old ones has been an interesting aspect of my work. Rocking-horses come in for a considerable amount of rough treatment, particularly those that are lodged in schools or hospitals, and it is very satisfying to take some decrepit old horse and repair and restore him to as good as new again.

It is always nice, too, to hear from other rocking-horse makers and from people who are just interested — sometimes the outcome can be quite extraordinary. One afternoon an elderly lady came to my workshop, just to have a look round. She made some complimentary remarks and then asked if I might be interested in her hair. Her hair? Why should I be interested in the short white hair of an elderly lady? But then she produced from her handbag a magnificent thick hank of auburn hair nearly two feet long. It transpired that she had had her beautiful hair cut in 1927 and kept it ever since. 'It's no good to me now, I thought you might like to make use of it for a rocking-horse!' I was later able to employ it in the restoration of a lovely little Victorian rocking-horse in which it perfectly matched the original hair.

1
WHY A ROCKING-HORSE?

This book is for people who like rocking-horses and who would like to make one. It is for people who like woodwork, but even if you have only dabbled at woodwork as a hobby there will be something here for you. The projects range from the simplest of plywood cut-out hobby-horses to a fully carved traditional style of rocking-horse. The making of the simple hobby-horse should be within the capability of almost anyone, while the fully carved horse, although considerably more complex and involved, is described in such a way that its construction should not present too many problems even for those people with limited tools and equipment at their disposal. The building of the fully carved horse does not require sophisticated or expensive machinery, but rather a degree of enthusiasm for the project — and perseverence. How to make a simple form of rocking-horse is also described; this is a rocker which in terms of ease of making lies between the simple hobby-horse and the fully carved rocking-horse. In addition, a chapter is devoted to the problems of renovating and restoring old and battered or broken rocking-horses.

This wooden animal has become, I admit, something of a consuming interest. It may seem odd that a man should spend a considerable proportion of his waking hours in the passionate pursuit of so unlikely a subject. Yet the rocking-horse is the most perfect of playthings. And should you have any doubts, perhaps I may dispel them and convey to you something of the fascination with which I regard this finest of toys.

Many supermarket entrances are graced with mechanically operated rocking spaceships, and a glance round the toy department of most large stores, or into any specialist toyshop, will reveal a wide range of rocking toys. You may find tiny wooden rockers with plywood heads, assemble-it-yourself plywood rocking constructions, tubular steel framed rocking-horses with plastic heads, tin or plastic horses mounted on dangerous looking springs, and rocking cradles, rocking boats, rocking motorbikes, rocking elephants, rocking anything. Many of these are lovely toys for toddlers but it seems to me that none of them is what could be called a *real* rocking-horse. Because a real rocking-horse (like Granny used to ride) is a proper looking horse mounted on curved bow rockers or a swing iron stand. He is wooden. He is painted (normally dapple grey). He has a real mane and tail and stirrups. He has glinting glass eyes that promise any child the ride of his life. And he is very big — to a small child he must seem enormous.

A number of shops display rocking-horses that seem to be all these things — but, beware. They may be made of glass reinforced plastic. There is nothing wrong with GRP (except the awful smell of raw resin) — some very good boats are made of the stuff. But wood has a much more sympathetic and unmistakable feel to it (even through paintwork). And rocking-horses should be individuals. How can a rocking-horse be individual when it comes out of a mould? No, it must be wooden and hand carved.

The traditional wooden rocking-horse occupies a very special place among playthings. His size, 'personality' and solidity set him apart from smaller toys. A child will develop a much more intimate relationship with a rocking-horse than with the large impersonal playground swings or seesaws. A rocking-horse can be a very real friend to a lonely child. He possesses, for the younger child, many of the qualities of a real horse, with none of the drawbacks. He never needs feeding or exercising on frosty winter mornings, he can look after himself and doesn't resent occasional neglect. He never needs to be 'mucked out'. And he is absolutely tireless; always ready to take the child rider on the most exciting, yet secure, imaginative gallops.

A wooden rocking-horse is much more than just a toy for the moment. He will outlast several generations of young riders. He will become a family heirloom and be passed down to new generations who will always greet him with delighted enthusiasm. And when, after many years of use, his mane and tail and saddle become tattered, his paintwork chipped and worn, and his mechanical parts rickety, he can be repaired and refurbished to give him a whole new lease of life.

It is strange how many adults are delighted by the idea of the rocking-horse. It seems to induce all sorts of nostalgic yearnings for the past — interestingly, whether or not one has owned or ridden a rocking-horse in childhood oneself. I must confess that I never had a rocking-horse as a child but I am making up for that deficiency now through all the rocking-horses that I make or restore. My own children are always ready to test ride a new horse (and they have one of their own, of course, as well), and I sometimes jump on and ride with them.

Once, when restoring an aged horse that had belonged to a school for many years, I came across an old gentleman in his seventies who remembered quite vividly having ridden that horse during his first day at school at the age of five. New children were apparently seated on the rocking-horse as a 'treat' when they were being introduced to the class. The clear memory of that initiation, and the rocking-horse, had remained with him for seventy years.

It is in the nature of things that toys are often roughly handled, and discarded when outgrown. So it is hardly surprising that relatively few toys survive from earlier periods. Also, because of their size, rocking-horses have never been greatly sought after as collectable items. Yet a few rocking-horses exist which date back to the early sixteenth century and small toy horses in clay, terracotta, or wood are known to have been used as playthings some three thousand years ago. It is easy to understand how small toys are discarded and lost. One would imagine, however, that it would be much harder to lose a thing the size of a rocking-horse. But this, too, does happen and I occasionally hear of rocking-horses having been 'found' after lying for years forgotten in attics or outbuildings.

Hobby-horses

Hobby-horses pre-date the rocking-horse by a long way and it is probable that children were playing with some simple form of this toy from very early times. Sometimes the term hobby-horse is used as synonymous with rocking-horse but I like to distinguish between the two in that whereas a rocking-horse is actually ridden — the child's feet are off the ground — the hobby-horse is normally held in one hand while the 'rider' runs about slapping a thigh to simulate the horse's gallop. The hobby-horse began as a plain stick bearing some simple representation of a horse's head. Occasionally a wheel was fixed to the lower end of the stick and this type became the commonest, the 'standard' hobby-horse, a good uncomplicated toy. Sometimes, with the addition of mane, reins and other accessories the simple idea of the hobby-horse became highly elaborate. The hobby-horse used by Morris dancers, for example, often involved a light frame of wickerwork over which was draped a cloth. It was strapped round the waist of the 'rider' (thus leaving both hands free), the large head pointing to the front, and the cloth reaching

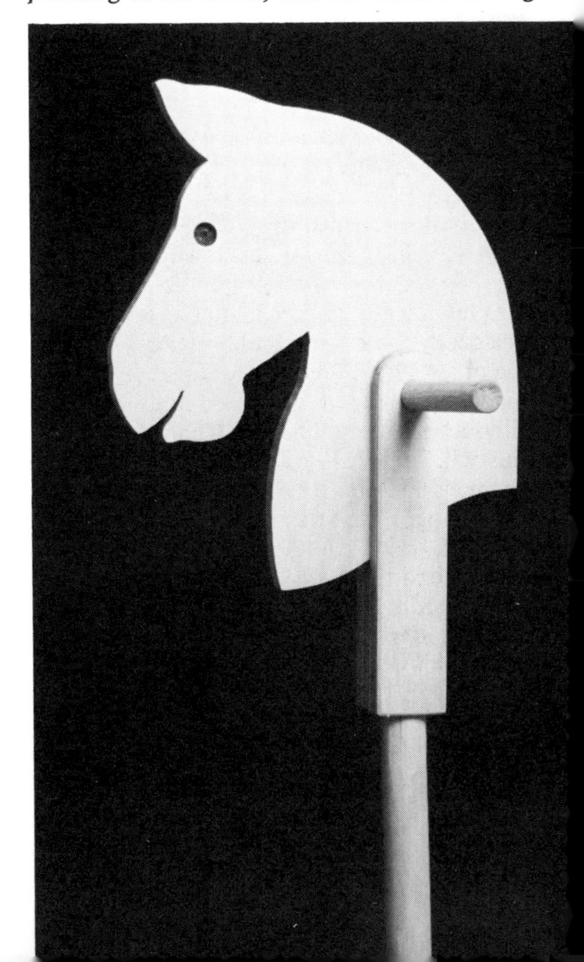

Plate 3 Simple plywood hobby-horse

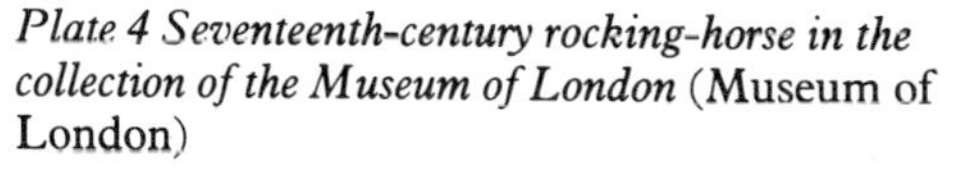

Plate 4 Seventeenth-century rocking-horse in the collection of the Museum of London (Museum of London)

almost to the ground all round to effectively conceal the 'rider's' legs. These hobby-horses are still used by modern Morris dancers and at first glance they can give a disconcerting impression of a real horse and rider, until you realise that the rider's waist disappears into the horse's back and that the 'horse' has but two legs.

The hobby-horse has a long history, but remains a popular toy today for younger children. Its great virtue is its simplicity and portability. Because it is of lightweight construction the head can be relatively large while still remaining manageable by even the smallest of children. Chapter 2 contains the designs for two simple hobby-horses consisting of a stick with head and wheel. The first is made of plywood with the head a cut-out silhouette shape (Plate 3). It is intended that this will be within the capability of virtually anyone and, with a little guidance in the sawing out and drilling, can be made by older children for their younger brothers or sisters. The second hobby-horse design has a head of solid wood which involves a little carving and shaping. For people who have done no carving before this could be a useful exercise.

Pull-along Horses

Toy horses of the pull-along type, the horse standing on a platform with little wheels, were known from very early times. They are usually small, too small to be ridden except by the tiniest children. But I have come across Victorian rocking-horses (of the straw-filled, hide-covered variety) in which the horse was mounted on a platform with wheels which was in turn fixed to the curved bow rockers with thumbscrews. The horse could thus be converted from rocking-horse to pull-along toy at will. Of course these horses are relatively light in weight but the problem with pull-along horses is that if you want to get on and ride you need someone else to pull you along. And if you are not a lightweight little toddler, the 'puller' is in for a tough job. But by mounting the toy horse on rockers the 'puller' is made redundant — all that is needed is you, your horse, and your imagination.

Early Rocking-horses

The earliest proper rocking-horses appear to have incorporated the kind of rockers which had long been used on rocking cradles for babies, with a hobby-horse type of head. The seventeenth-century rocking-horse in the Museum of London has curved rockers of solid timber pegged through to cross pieces which are angled inwards towards the seat to give the typical boat-shaped appearance (Plate 4). At each extremity of the rockers a semi-circle of timber projects which acts as a stop; the horse could rock so far but no farther. This feature is retained in some form in all later variations on the same bow rocker theme, and is vital. A rocking-horse will be a heavy construction and there must be no possibility of it overturning on top of its rider. (Sadly, some modern manufacturers ignore this well tried and tested feature, apparently relying on the lightness of the construction of their horse, padded and fabric covered etc, to avoid injury when they overturn.)

The head of the Museum of London horse is a shaped solid block, simply carved. The weight of this head is partly counterbalanced by a solid wooden rump. The seat is narrow and was once padded with horsehair and leather covered. Two shaped pieces of wood form the front and back of the saddle and a foot rest is provided at each side. The remains of the original paintwork cling forlornly to the well worn wood.

It is upon this style of early rocking-horse that the project described in Chapter 3 is based. It is quite straightforward to make, being smaller and lighter than the original, and employing plywood rocker panels rather than solid timber. There is a choice of three heads for which instructions are given: a simple cut-out silhouette; one involving some carving and shaping; the third more fully carved (Plates 5, 6 and 7). The heads are interchangeable on the same base to enable you to choose whichever you feel best able to tackle.

Fully Carved Rocking-horses

I sometimes wonder if the maker of the first proper rocking-horse had any inkling of what a perfect toy he was creating and that more than three hundred years later the same basic formula would still be bringing delight to countless thousands of children. By mounting the toy horse on rockers it became possible for the horse to have a movement akin to the motion of a real horse, and for it to be easily controllable by a single child rider. A large wooden rocking-horse can weigh up to a

Plate 5 Cut-out silhouette head for the simple rocking-horse

Plate 6 Fully carved head with glass eyes for the simple rocking-horse

Plate 7 The completed simple plywood rocking-horse, showing the more lightly carved head and painted finish

hundred pounds or more, and yet be managed by a tiny child. Also, the movement can be varied at will from a gentle to-and-fro to an exhilarating gallop. There is no complex mechanism to break down; no knobs or wires or strings; no batteries; just a little muscular effort is all the motive power required.

It was not too long after the advent of the first slab-sided rocking-horses that fully carved horses began to be made, and a few very fine examples survive of horses beautifully carved in great detail. Some of these early horses needed extra supporting struts which were fixed under the belly. But most came to be made in the familiar way with the four legs wholly supporting the weight of the horse and rider. The legs are splayed out at full reach back and front, the hooves being bolted onto the rockers at each side, or onto cross pieces between the rockers. The rockers themselves became long, thin graceful arcs of timber, angled inwards to converge at the ends where turned cross pieces were fitted. The platform in the middle, as well as being an essential part of the construction of the rockers, provided a step up to the horse. Occasionally these rocking-horses were extremely large, and some had a small seat fixed at each end of the rockers so that three children could ride simultaneously.

Through the nineteenth century the wooden rocking-horse became the characteristic toy of the nursery. Rocking-horse making flourished and a number of wooden rocking-horse factories were established. A few of these survived until quite recently and though they may have produced some fine examples in their time, it must be said that their later products are often rather poorly made and carved.

Many attempts were made to devise 'new and improved' rocking mechanisms with the use of springs or levers, and the velocipede, a sort of rocking-horse tricycle, should be mentioned, but the traditional curved bow rockers remained the standard and best form of mounting until the introduction of the steel swing iron safety stand in 1880. This arrangement was so successful it largely superseded the bow rocker. It gives an effective motion to

Plate 8 The large and small fully carved rocking horses which are described in detail in Chapter 4

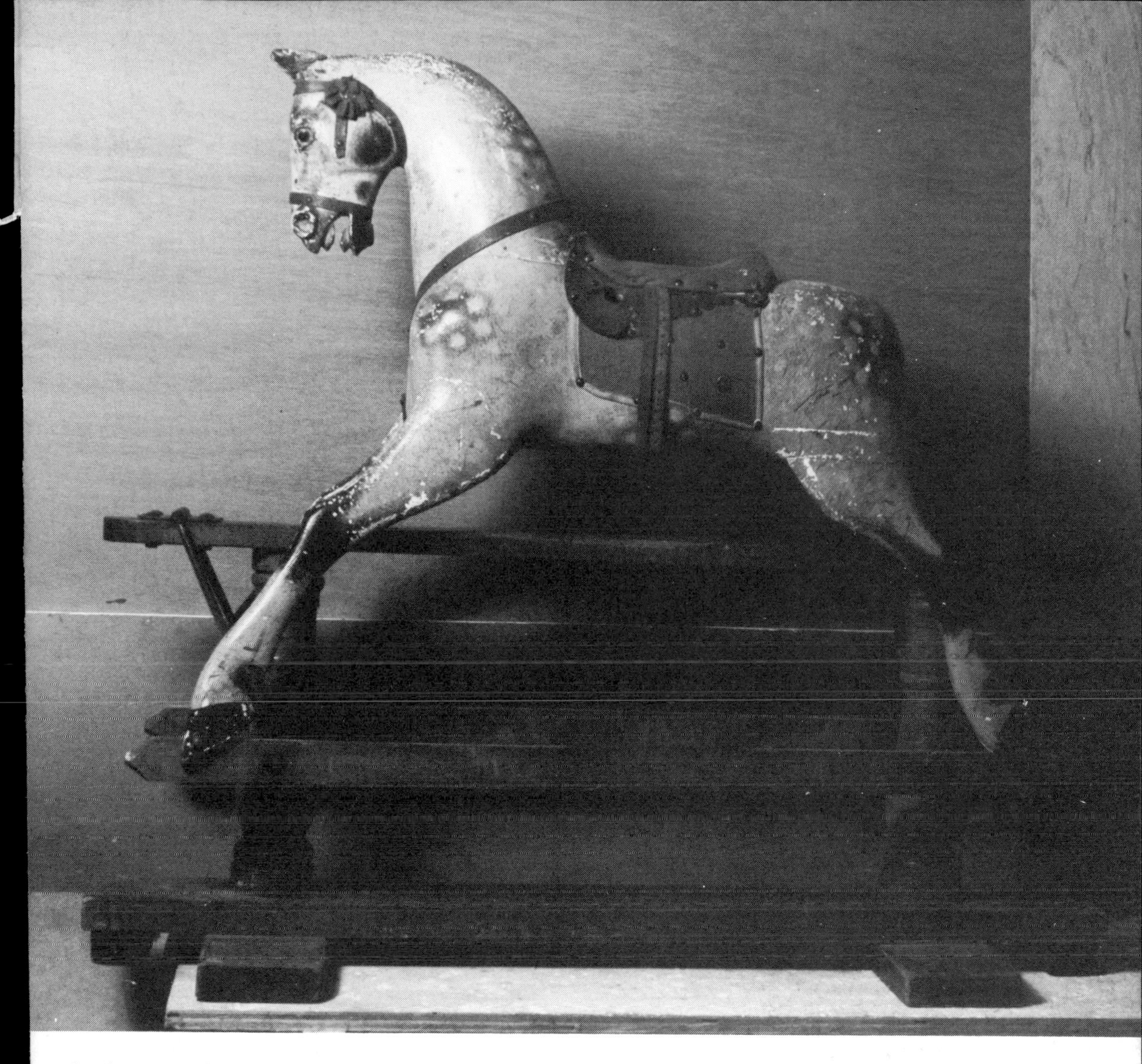

Plate 9 A well used, well loved old rocking-horse in need of renovation

the horse and an equally exciting ride. It is immune from tipping over, being so arranged that the horse will rock only so far and no farther. But its safety aspect is important not so much for the rider, but for children who stand too close to the horse being ridden. A child who gets too close to a swing iron mounted horse in motion may well be bumped by it — and that can hurt — but he will not get his toes crushed, which *will* happen if he gets too close to a moving bow rocker mounted horse. In addition, bow rockers on a large horse take up a great deal of space, far more than an equal sized horse on a swing iron stand; and bow rockers do move about on the floor so that the ends will eventually gouge lumps out of the walls or furniture.

Having said that, I do think that curved bow rockers look beautiful — the fine lines of the horse are uncluttered by the stand. The small fully carved rocking-horse described in Chapter 4 is therefore mounted on bow rockers, while the large model has a swing iron stand (Plate 8).

These two fully carved horses are very traditional in style and construction but the particular method of construction described is especially suitable for people with a fairly limited tool chest. Although a machine such as a band-saw, for example, will greatly facilitate the cutting out of the various shapes, a lack of this machine should not deter anyone keen to have a go. Remember these rocking-horses are *hand* crafted. A lot of people, some with only modest woodworking skills, have built beautiful rocking-horses though at the outset they may well have been rather doubtful about their capacity to do the job. And there is no doubt that to have your children and grandchildren riding a rocking-horse of your own construction is a special source of satisfaction.

The making of a traditional wooden rocking-horse involves a number of skills and it is this variety of work that renders rocking-horse making so satisfactory an occupation. The building of the stand or rockers and the assembly of the various parts of the horse involve basic joinery and wood-turning, then carving. The horse is covered with gesso — a peculiar skill. It is painted and hand finished. The harness and saddle are hand made of real leather. The steel parts, bits, swing irons etc, involve some metalworking. To be an all-in-one rocking-horse maker then, you need to apply yourself to some of the skills of joiner, carver, gessoer, painter, leatherworker and blacksmith. In Chapter 4, each of these processes is described and information is given about tackling these various aspects of the construction. The list of skills is not as formidable as it may first appear, however, and I hope that with the help of the information given you will be well equipped to have a go at one of these fascinating projects. To anyone with the urge to build a real rocking-horse, and who is reasonably competent with his or her hands, I would say 'give it a try'. You will almost certainly surprise yourself in a most pleasing way.

Plate 10 The same horse as in Plate 9 — after treatment

Renovating Old Rocking-horses

Old rocking-horses quite often come up for sale at auctions, and can sometimes be acquired from junk shops relatively cheaply, or even be given, which is better. And often, when outgrown, an old rocking-horse will be

Plate 11 A particularly fine rocking-horse after renovation

put aside into an attic or shed against the advent of a new generation of children. When the time comes to bring him into use again the magnificent steed which memory recalls is found to be a hairless, saddle-less, chipped, broken and shabby creature. It is for people presented with the problem of what to do with such a sorry old horse that Chapter 5 is intended.

Old rocking-horses come in great variety, not only of shapes, styles and mountings, but also of construction methods, carving and accessories and fittings. The best are truly fine examples of workmanship and artistry, despite their superficial shabbiness and signs of wear and tear. But it must be said that some are very poorly made and crudely carved, and cause a lot of headaches in the renovation. It is always worthwhile, however, if you can give some tired and neglected old nag a whole new lease of life and send him back to where he rightly belongs — the nursery. Old rocking-horses, or new ones for that matter, seem wasted if they are to be seen only as relics of a lost past, as museum pieces, or as untouchable items of valued furniture. To be the willing transport for a child's imagination and pleasure is, after all, what a rocking-horse is for.

But there are exceptions. Occasionally one does come across an old rocking-horse in its original paintwork and tack, or a hide-covered horse, very battered and worn perhaps, but an excellent example of a typical antique style of rocking-horse. In this case it may be preferable to restore the horse only minimally, if at all, since it may be that in doing so one would be destroying something of particular antique value.

2
TWO HOBBY-HORSES

The Plywood Hobby-horse

The Tools Required
Fretsaw or coping saw
Smoothing plane
Brace, plus 3/8in (10mm), 1/2in (13mm), 3/4in (18mm) twist bits (or an electric drill and flat bits)
2 or 3 small G cramps
PVA or other good wood glue
Fine glass or garnet paper

A piece of 3/8in (9mm or 10mm) birch plywood, measuring 10in x 15½in (255mm x 395mm), will be sufficient for head, wheel and connecting pieces.

Cutting List

	Thickness x Width x Length	*Wood*
Head connecting piece	3/8 x 1 1/8 x 15½in (10 x 30 x 395mm)	Plywood
Head	3/8 x 7 x 8½in (10 x 180 x 216mm)	Plywood
Handle	½in(dia.) x 7in (13 x 178mm)	Dowel (ramin)
Stick	¾in(dia.) x 28in (19 x 711mm)	Dowel (ramin)
Wheel	3/8 x 4 x 4in (10 x 105 x 105mm)	Plywood
Wheel connecting piece	3/8 x 1 1/8 x 14½in (10 x 30 x 368mm)	Plywood
Axle	½in(dia.) x 1¼in (13 x 32mm)	Dowel (ramin)

This simple hobby-horse, with a plywood cut-out silhouette shape of a horse's head mounted on a dowel stick with a plywood wheel at the bottom, should present few difficulties in the making.

The head shape (see Fig 1) should be drawn out full size on a piece of stiff paper to be used as a pattern. This is then drawn round on the plywood and cut out using either a fretsaw or coping saw, and the edges sanded smooth. The eyes are marked by drilling part way into the plywood from either side with a 3/8in (10mm) drill bit (ideally a forstner bit because this leaves a clean, neat, flat-bottomed hole). The wheel is drawn onto the plywood with a pair of compasses set at radius 2in (50mm) and similarly cut out and sanded (Plate 12).

Next cut some strips of plywood for the pieces which will be needed to connect the head and wheel to the stick. These two con-

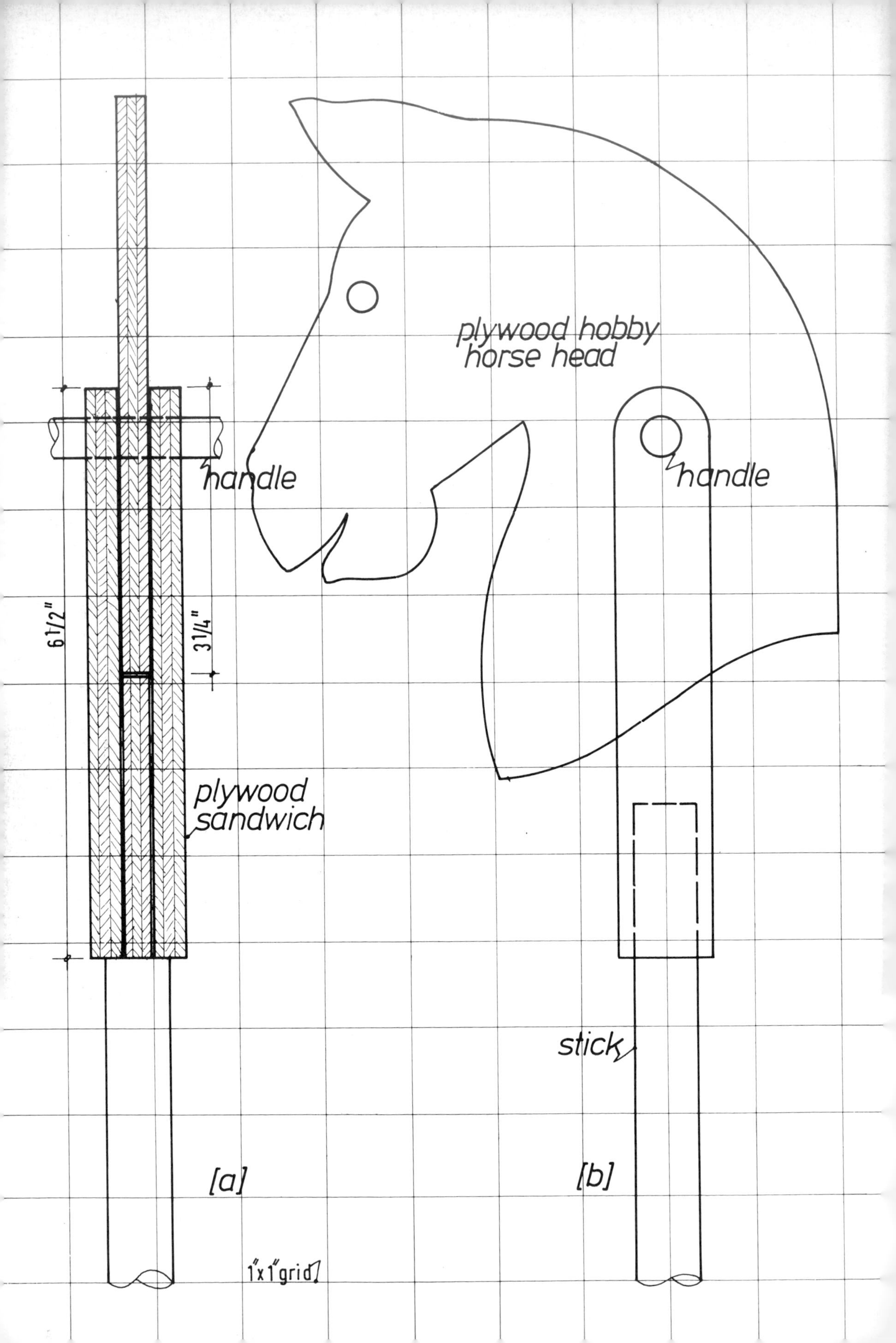
plywood hobby horse head
handle
handle
6 1/2"
3 1/4"
plywood sandwich
stick
[a]
[b]
1"x1" grid

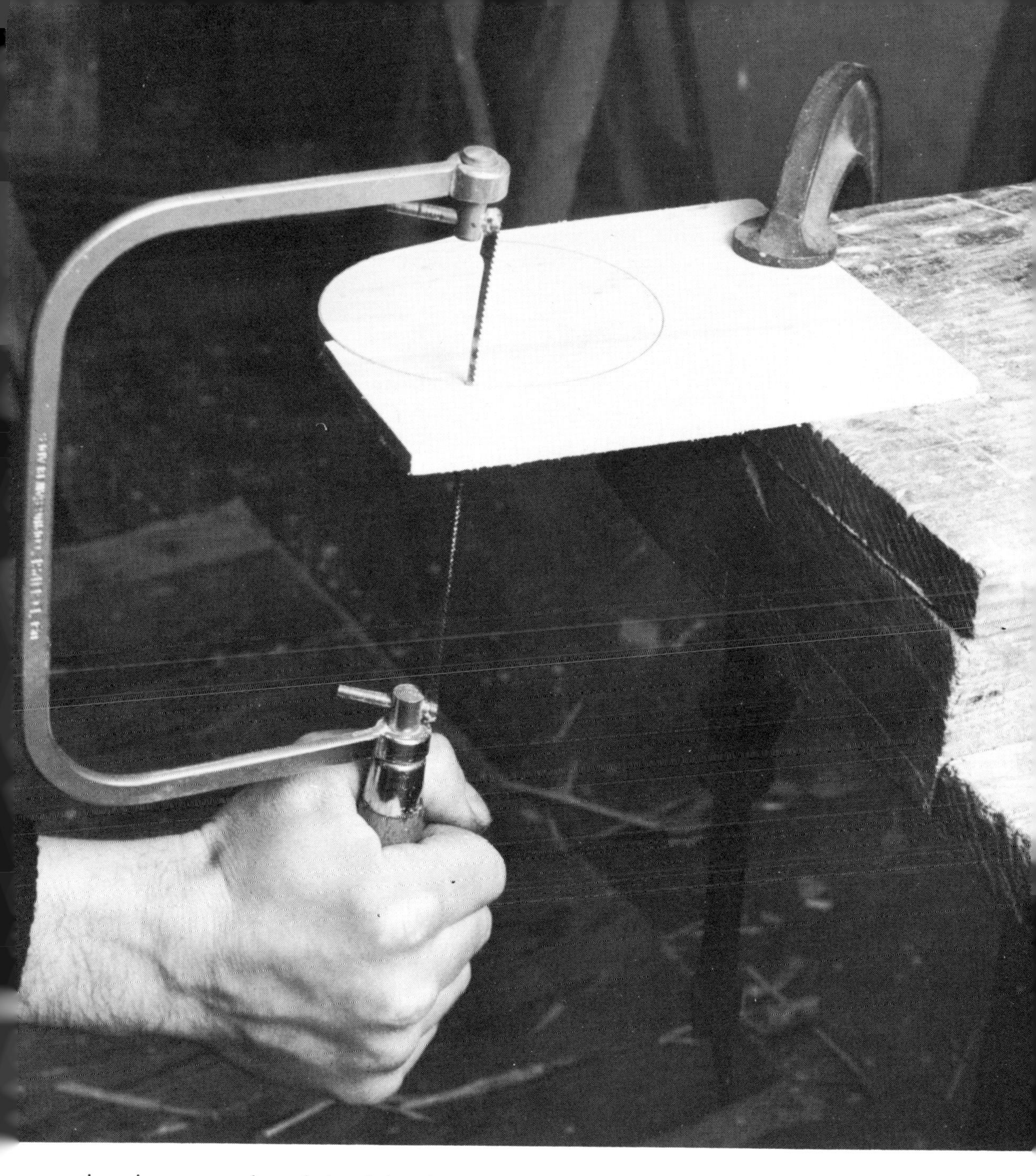

Plate 12 Cutting out the hobby-horse's plywood wheel with a coping saw

necting pieces are each made by gluing three strips of plywood together to form a sort of bridle joint which slots over the head and wheel, as shown in the scale drawings. These strips should initially be cut rather wider than required so that after they are joined together, by gluing and cramping, they can be planed down to finish about 1⅛in (30mm) square.

Fig 1 Scale drawing of plywood hobby-horse head

The middle strip of the head connecting piece should be cut to fit snugly against the underside of the head before gluing up. The two outer strips can be rounded off at the top ends as shown in Plate 13; the other end is cut off square and the centre marked (by drawing two diagonals) for drilling the hole into which the

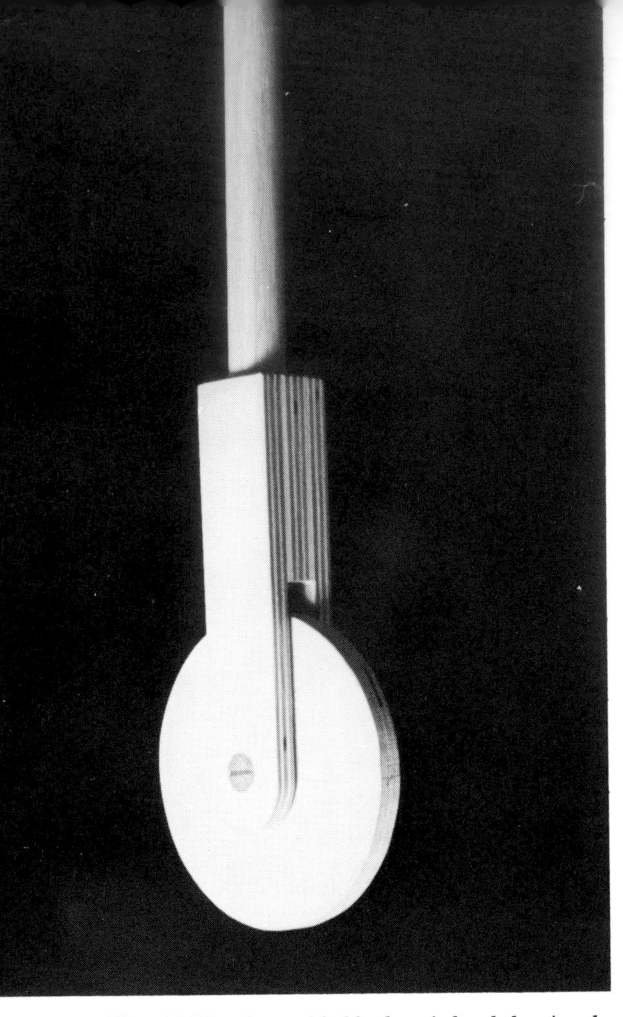

Plate 13 The plywood hobby-horse's head showing the plywood 'sandwich' which connects the head to the stick

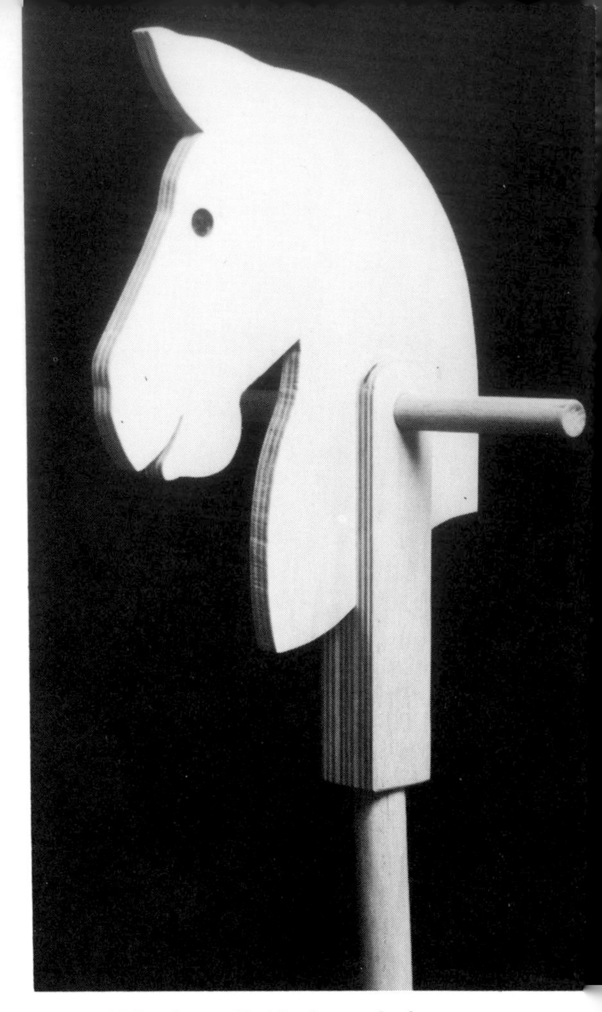

Plate 14 The plywood hobby-horse wheel arrangement. Note the wedge which secures the axle at each end

stick will be glued. When drilling the stick hole it is as well to hold the connecting piece firmly in a vice to prevent it splitting under the pressure of the ¾in (18mm) bit, and try to drill the hole as straight as you can to a depth of about 1¾in (45mm).

The wheel connecting piece is similarly squared off and drilled for the stick and the lower ends can be rounded off as shown (see Fig 2). Mark the position of the centre of the hole for the axle and drill through, first tucking a piece of scrap plywood into the bridle joint where the wheel will go. A pillar or stand drill will best ensure that the hole goes through exactly at right angles, and while the ½in (13mm) bit is in the drill the wheel hole can be drilled, and also the hole through the head to take the handle. The wheel will need to spin freely, so the hole in the wheel needs to be filed out slightly so that it spins on the axle, and the inner faces of the bridle joint either sanded down or pared down with a sharp chisel to allow the wheel to slot in easily without binding. The dowel handle is pushed into its hole and glued in position centrally. It can be rounded off at the ends. A short piece of ½in (13mm) dowel is cut for the axle, and pushed through the holes in the wheel connecting piece and the wheel itself, and glued in place at each end. Avoid getting any glue on the wheel or you may inadvertently glue it rigid! The axle is best fixed by making a thin saw cut into each end, and wedging it in place (see Plate 14). Let the glue dry, sand the hobby-horse down, and varnish or paint according to whim.

Fig 2 Scale drawing of plywood hobby-horse wheel arrangement. Note that the inside faces of the bridle in (a) are pared away with a sharp chisel to enable the wheel to spin freely and that the axle (c) is secured with two small wedges

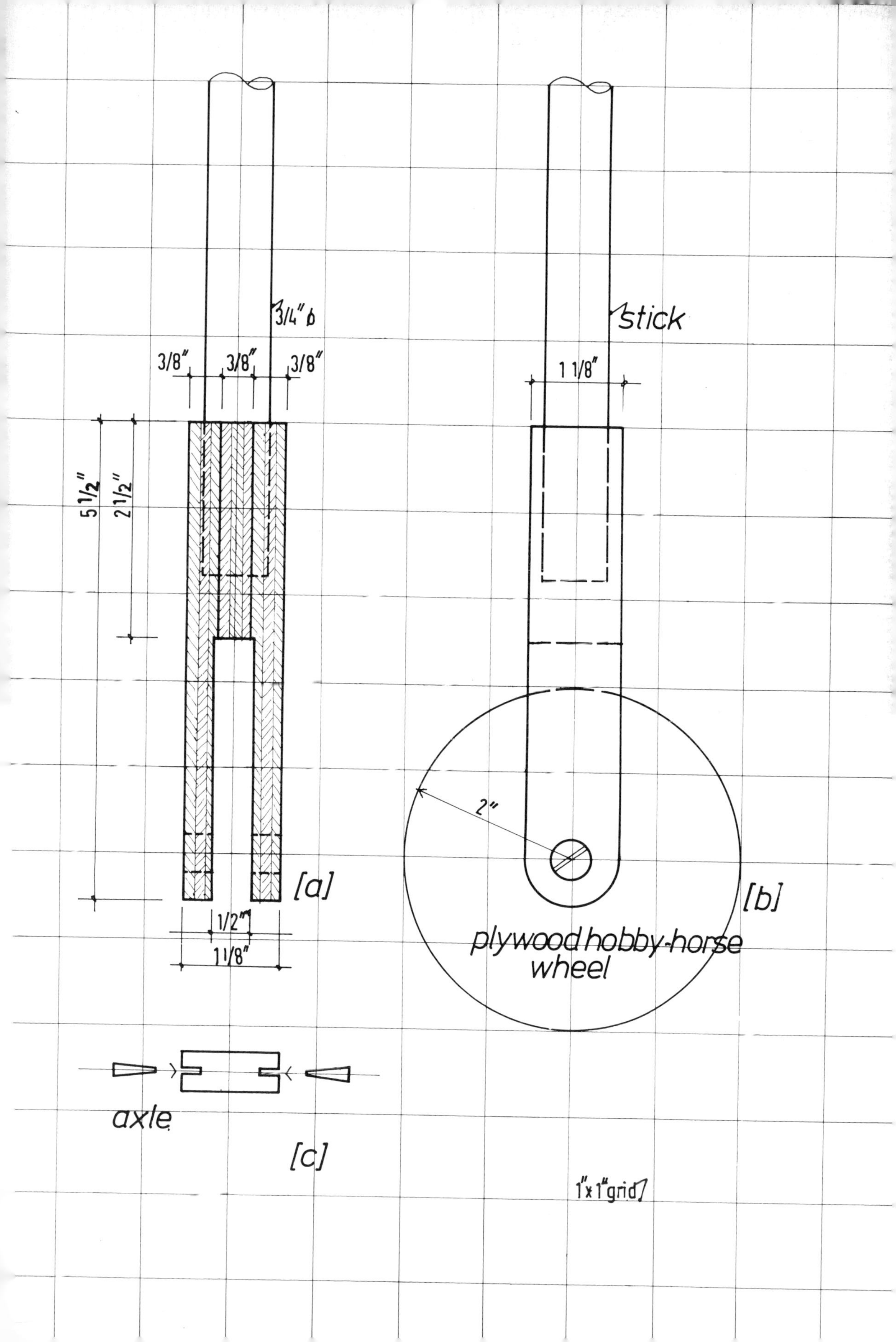
3/4" ⌀
stick
3/8"
3/8"
3/8"
1 1/8"
5 1/2"
2 1/2"
[a]
1/2"
1 1/8"
2"
[b]
plywood hobby-horse wheel
axle
[c]
1"x 1" grid

The Solid Head Hobby-horse

The Tools Required
Coping saw and/or jigsaw
½in (13mm) bevel-edged chisel
1in (25mm) bevel-edged chisel
Brace, plus ½in (13mm), ⅝in (16mm) and ⅞in (21mm) twist bits (or electric drill and flat bits)
A spokeshave would be useful

Cutting List

	Thickness x Width x Length	*Wood*
Head	1½ x 5½ x 8in (38 x 140 x 205mm)	Beech or other
Handle	½in(dia.) x 7½in (13 x 190mm)	Dowel (ramin)
Stick	⅞in(dia.) x 28in (22 x 711mm)	Dowel (ramin)
Wheel	⅜ x 4 x 4in (10 x 105 x 105mm)	Plywood
Wheel connecting piece	1½ x 1½ x 5½in (38 x 38 x 140mm)	Beech or other
Axle	½in(dia.) x 1⅝in (13mm x 41mm)	Dowel (ramin)

This hobby-horse has a solid wooden head and wheel connecting piece, rather than plywood, and consequently requires a little carving. The shaping of the head can be accomplished entirely with the two flat chisels with the additional help, perhaps, of a spokeshave and a sharp penknife (Fig 3c). You will see that this one again uses dowel (ramin) for the stick (diameter ⅞in (22mm) this time), handles and axle, and has a wheel cut from ⅜in (10mm) plywood of radius 2in (50mm). For a better finish the wheel could be made of a wood to match the head. With the exception of the dowel which was bought 'off the shelf', the parts of the hobby-horse illustrated here are offcuts purchased from a timber merchant for just a few pence. I used beech for the head and the wheel connecting piece, but many other woods would do as well, bearing in mind that a hobby-horse comes in for a very rough ride when in use, so it needs to be tough.

The wheel connecting piece is made from a 1½in (38mm) square block rounded off at the lower end and slotted to take the wheel (Fig 4). I made the slot ¹¹⁄₁₆in (17mm) wide on mine by first drilling a ⅞in (16mm) hole through the piece centrally, sawing out the bridle and tidying it up with a sharp chisel. A couple of large thin washers at each side of the wheel keep the wheel central and prevent it from rubbing against the sides of the slot. The upper end is marked and drilled for the stick with the ⅞in (21mm) bit, which penetrates about 1¾in (45mm) and is finished with a chamfer at each corner as shown in Plates 15 and 16. The wheel axle is glued in place and secured with small wedges tapped into saw cuts at either end as shown in Fig 4.

The head is drawn full size onto the wood (Fig 3) and is cut out using a coping saw. A jigsaw (saber saw), or band-saw if you have one, will make lighter work of this. The holes for

Fig 3 Scale drawing of the solid head hobby-horse head. The areas which are rounded off or shaped are shown in (c) (not to scale)

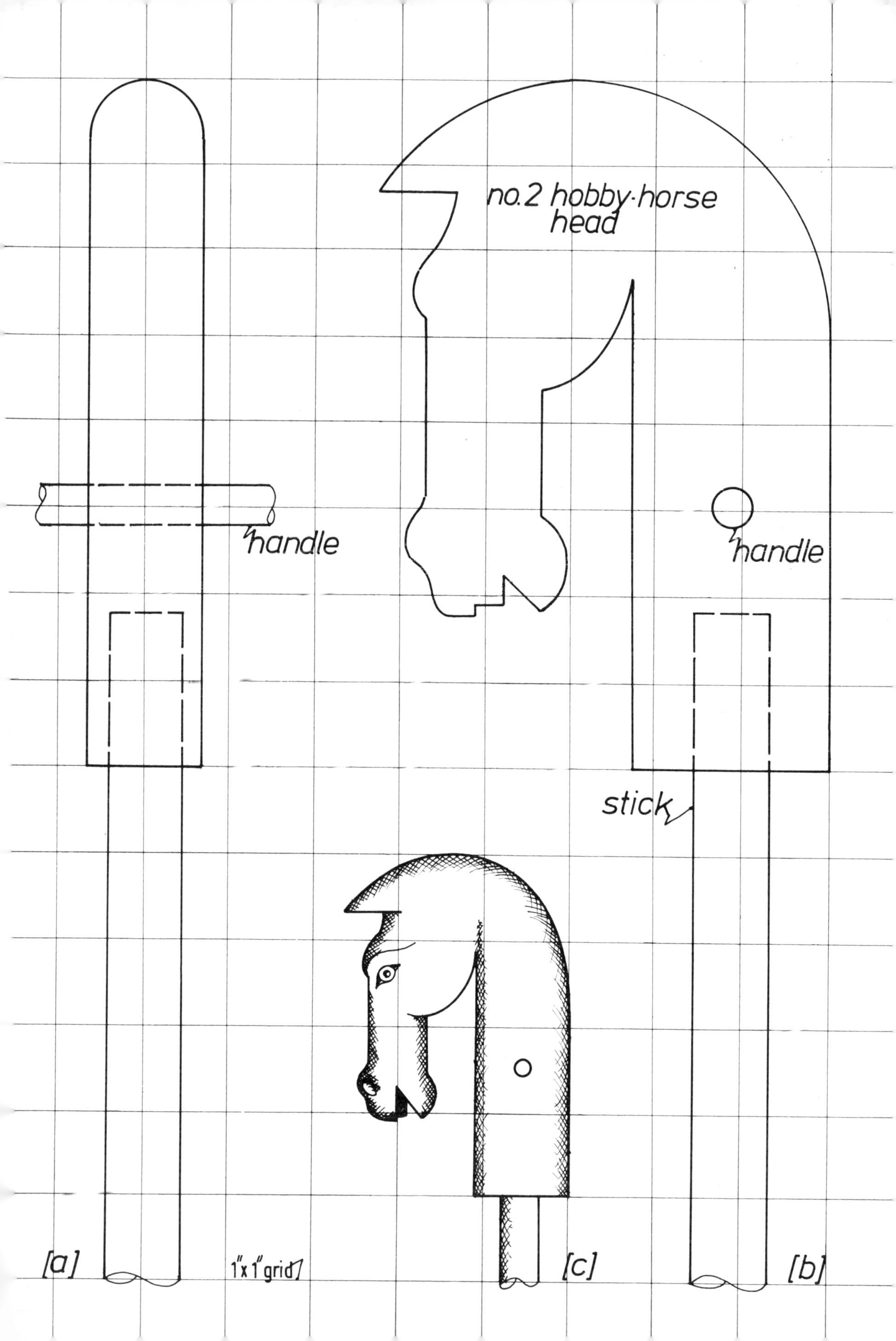
no.2 hobby-horse head
handle
handle
stick
[a]
1"x 1" grid
[c]
[b]

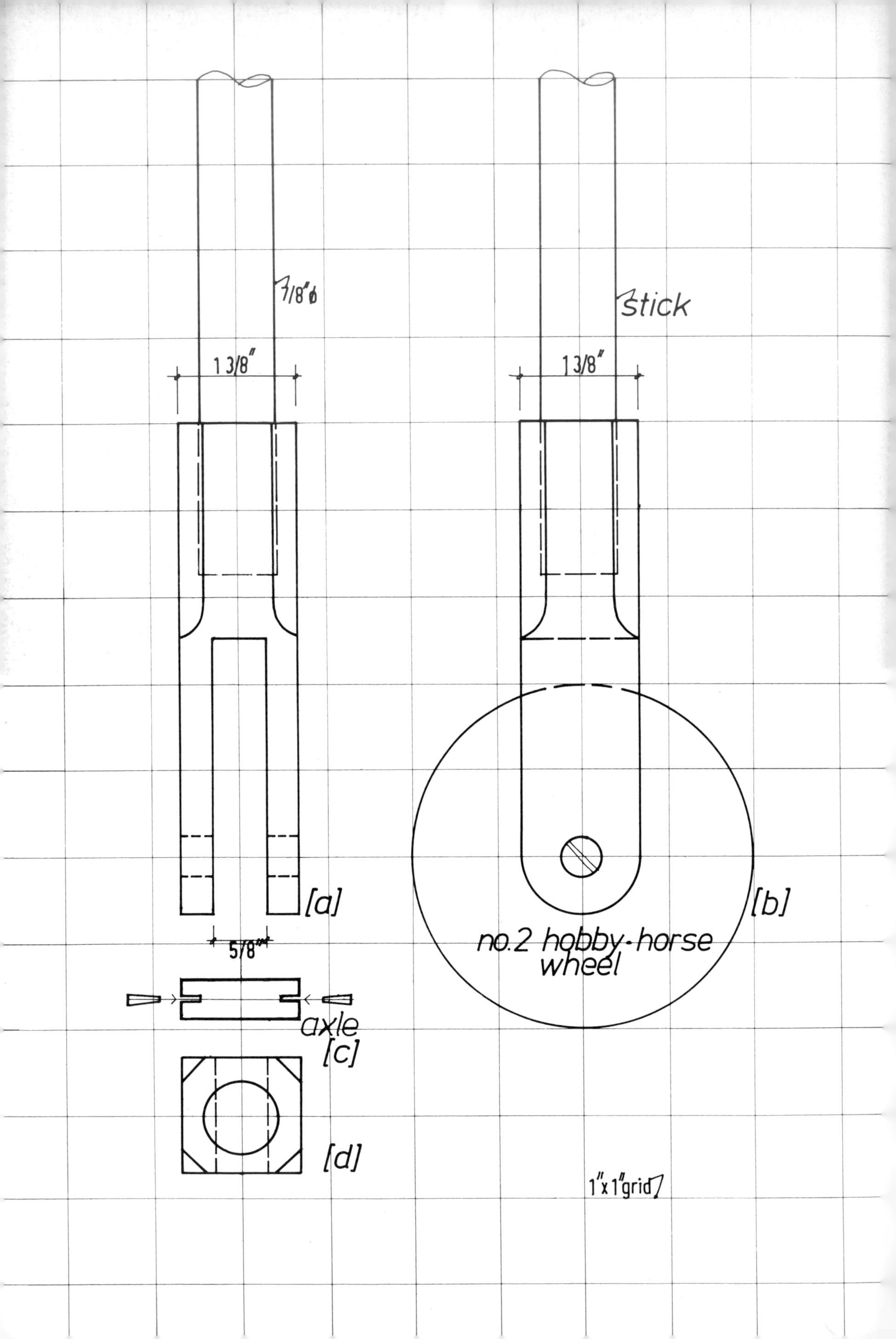

7/8"ø
stick
1 3/8"
1 3/8"
[a]
[b]
5/8"
no.2 hobby-horse wheel
axle
[c]
[d]
1"x1" grid

Plates 15 and 16 The solid head hobby-horse wheel arrangement. Note how the connecting piece is chamfered, and the wedging of the axle

the stick and handle are drilled with the 7/8in (21mm) bit and 1/2in (13mm) bit respectively. The shaping of the head consists of rounding off the square edges over the top of the head and down the neck. The spokeshave is useful for this. The lower part of the head and round the mouth are also rounded with a 1in (25mm) chisel, but the nostrils and 'eyebrows' should be left fairly proud. The mouth is cut in slightly with a 1/2in (13mm) chisel to suggest the teeth and the nostrils can be hollowed out a little if you have a small gouge. The eyes are cut in shallow relief with the point of a penknife, and can be coloured in or painted if desired. When sanding down, round off any sharp corners, particularly at the bottom of the neck.

The shape of the head of this hobby-horse is perhaps a little idiosyncratic but it is easy to make and looks attractive. You could 'separate' the ears with a coping saw and decorate the head with coloured ribbons. The whole thing could well be painted in any colour scheme you fancy — but of course paint does tend to chip when the hobby-horse is hurled about the garden, as it will be, so after the final sanding down and gluing together it is probably best to varnish.

Fig 4 Scale drawing of the solid head hobby-horse wheel arrangement. The axle (c) is secured with two small wedges and (d) shows a plan of the connecting piece

The length of stick indicated in the cutting list is suitable for a child of four or five years old — for younger children the stick should be shortened appropriately.

There is a wide range of possibilities of development from the basic hobby-horse on a stick idea. Employing twin wheels at the bottom solves the problem (if it is one) of making a bridle joint or slot for the wheel to run in. The head can range from the simplest of cut-out silhouettes to one elaborately carved in the round complete with mane and reins. However it is done though, you can be sure that the children will gain an enormous amount of pleasure from riding it.

Plates 17 and 18 The solid head hobby-horse showing the way the head is rounded off over the top and down the neck. Note the dowel handle which passes tight through the neck. This head is varnished and the eyes and ears coloured in with black paint

3
THE SIMPLE ROCKING-HORSE

This small rocking-horse is designed to be made by the novice woodworker. Its small size and lightweight construction mean that it is easy to manipulate the parts while it is being made and, after completion, light enough to carry without effort from one room to another. It is suitable for children up to about three years old but there seems no reason why a larger version could not be tackled, by scaling up the plans appropriately, which would suit rather older children. Though light, it is solidly constructed so will stand up to the hard wear and tear to which all rocking-horses are subject. No difficult woodwork joints are used — the parts are all butt jointed together, glued and screwed. Three different heads are described which can be fitted onto the same rocker arrangement. The first is a simple cut-out silhouette of the horse's head; the second employs some simple carving; the third is more completely carved. I suggest you choose whichever head you feel best able to tackle.

The Tools Required

Jigsaw (saber saw)
Coping saw
Smoothing plane
Spokeshave (not vital but very useful)
Hand or electric drill and 5/32in (4mm) twist drill and countersink bit
Brace with 3/4in (18mm) twist bit (or electric drill and flat bit)
Screwdriver and thirty-nine 1in (25mm) x 8 gauge countersunk wood screws
PVA or any good carpenter's glue
For the Mark 2 and Mark 3 heads 1/2in (13mm) and 1in (25mm) carving gouges, and 1/4in (6mm), 1/2in (13mm) and 1in (25mm) bevel-edged chisels will be needed

Cutting List

Each piece is listed individually below, but a piece of 3/8in (10mm) plywood, 33in x 36in (838mm x 914mm), is ample to cut all the ply parts.

	Thickness x Width x Length	*Wood*
Rocker side panels x 2	3/8 x 12 x 36in (each) (10 x 305 x 914mm)	Birch plywood
Rocker end cross pieces x 2	3/4 x 8 3/4 x 10 1/4in (each) (18 x 222 x 260mm)	Blockboard
Seat	3/8 x 8 x 19 1/8in (10 x 203 x 486mm)	Plywood
Battens x 2	1 x 2 x 15 1/2in (each) (25 x 50 x 394mm)	Redwood
Seat back x 2	3/8 x 6 1/2 x 6in (each) (10 x 165 x 152mm)	Plywood
Rump piece	2 x 3 x 5 1/2in (50 x 75 x 140mm)	Jelutong or similar
Foot rests	1 x 3 x 14in (25 x 75 x 360mm)	Beech or similar

	Heads	
'Mark 1' head	1½ x 8½ x 8¾in (38 x 216 x 222mm)	Jelutong or similar
handle	¾in(dia.) x 7in (19 x 178mm)	Dowel
'Mark 2' head	2 x 8 x 11¾in (50 x 203 x 300mm)	Jelutong or similar
muscle blocks x 2	1 x 6 x 15in (both) (25 x 152 x 381mm)	Jelutong or similar
handles x 2	1in(dia.) x 4in (each, for turning) (25 x 102mm)	Beech or similar
'Mark 3' head	2 x 8¼ x 11¾in (50 x 210 x 300mm)	Jelutong or similar
muscle blocks x 2	1½ x 6 x 15in (both) (38 x 152 x 381mm)	Jelutong or similar
eye & ear pieces	½ x 2 x 10in (13 x 51 x 254mm)	Jelutong or similar

The Rocker Base

First draw out the shapes of the various parts full size on stiff paper to be used as patterns. (Incidentally, full-size paper patterns for this rocking-horse are available, see Appendix 3 for address.) The rocker side panels and the seat are of ⅜in (10mm) plywood and these can be drawn onto the plywood first (Fig 5). It simplifies things if you mark the positions of all the screw holes on the paper patterns so that these can be pricked through the paper into the plywood at the same time as marking out the side panels. The side panels are then cut out using a jigsaw (saber saw) (Plate 19). These two panels need to be exactly the same, so clamp them together and smooth along the curves with sandpaper wrapped around a block, or better still use a spokeshave. You can clamp the two panels together with G cramps (first protecting the surfaces of the plywood with a couple of pieces of scrap wood at each cramp). But if you do not have any cramps the two panels can be temporarily screwed together using three or four screws through the positions of the screw holes already marked. When smoothing off the bottom curve of the rocker panels ensure, by running your fingers along the curve, that they are even and without bumps.

Next drill out the screw holes and countersink them so that the screw heads will sit just below the surface of the wood. The holes are all countersunk from the outside face with the exception of the three holes through which each foot rest will be fixed, which are countersunk from the inside. It is as well to mark the panels 'left' and 'right' appropriately with a pencil to avoid getting them mixed up. On the inside of each of the panels mark the positions of the two cross pieces which run at right angles to the top straight edge of the rocker panels. These two cross pieces are of ¾in (18mm) blockboard and can be drawn and cut out next. (You can make them from the same ⅜in (10mm) plywood as the rest if you like, but in this case you will need extra battens to the joins on the inside.) The side and top edges should be planed straight and square.

Fig 5 Scale drawing of simple rocking-horse rocker side panel

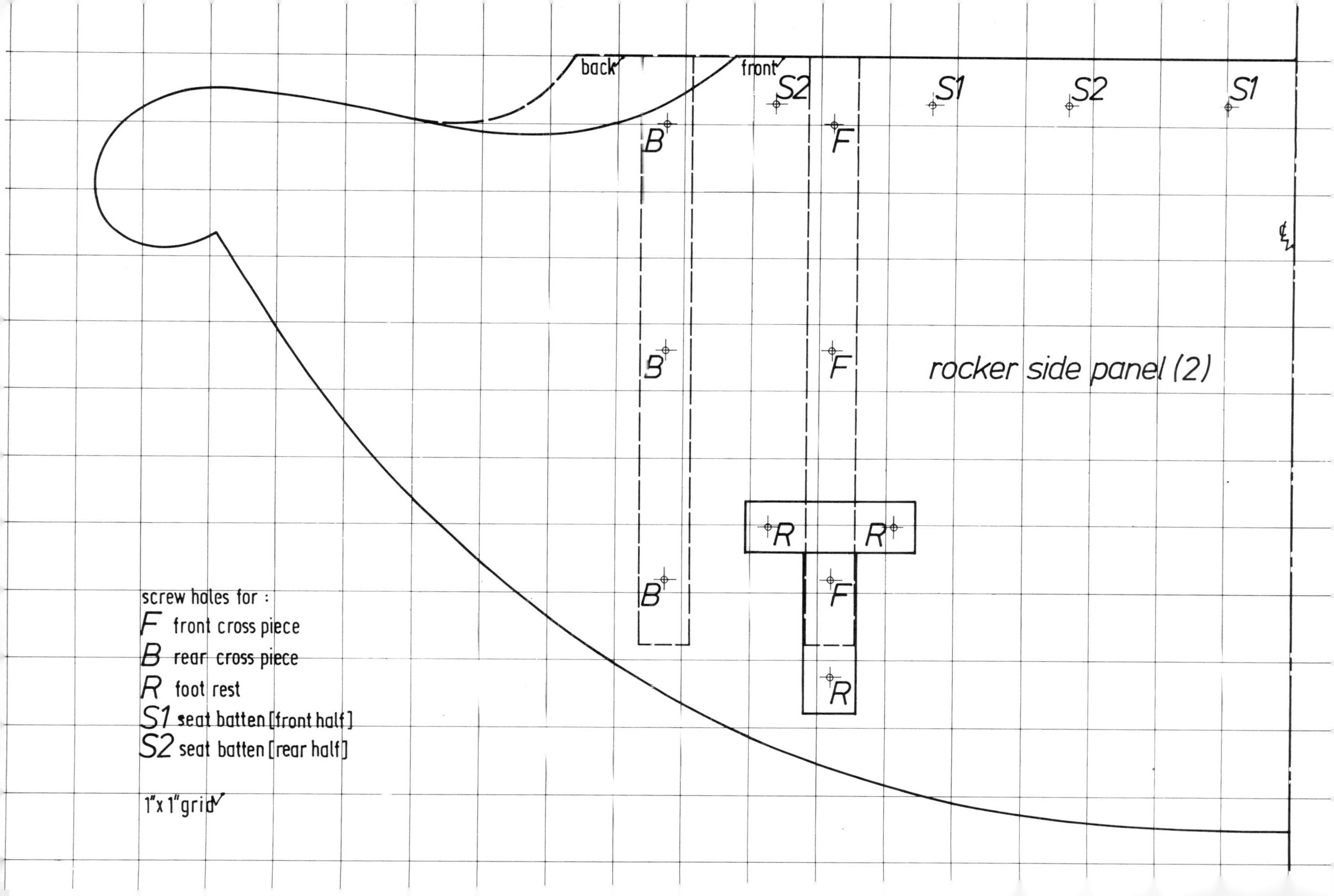
back
front
S2
S1
S2
S1
B
B
B
F
F
F
R
R
R
rocker side panel (2)
screw holes for :
F front cross piece
B rear cross piece
R foot rest
S1 seat batten [front half]
S2 seat batten [rear half]
1"x 1" grid

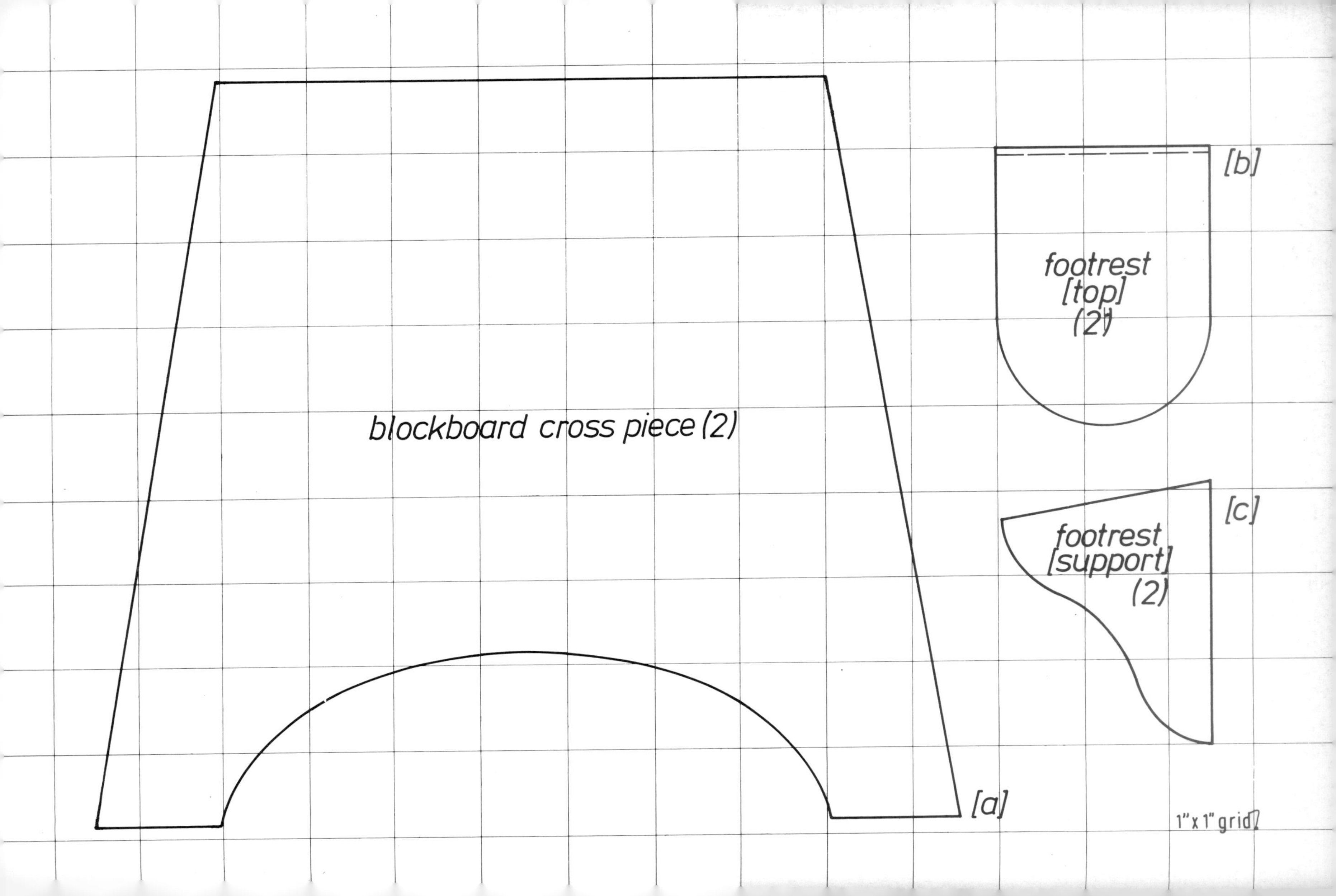
blockboard cross piece (2)
[a]
[b]
footrest
[top]
(2)
[c]
footrest
[support]
(2)
1" x 1" grid

The two battens to which the seat will be screwed are glued and screwed in position on the inside of each of the rocker side panels. They should project above the straight top edge of the panels by about 3/16in (5mm) because these edges are to be bevelled with the smoothing plane to allow the seat to fit snugly down onto the rockers (Plate 20). The bevels are marked by holding one of the cross pieces up to the end of the batten, level with the inside corner of the top of the side panel, and drawing along the upper edge of the cross piece with a sharp pencil. Carefully plane down the angle of the bevel until you reach this mark.

The two cross pieces are glued and screwed in place (Plate 21). Make sure that the top edges of the cross pieces and the side panels are level. It is a good idea to lightly spokeshave a little wood from the inner lower edges of the rocker side panels to form a bevel that lets the rockers sit flat to the floor. Cut the seat slightly wider than required and mark and drill its screw holes — four are sufficient, two each

Fig 6 Scale drawing of simple rocking-horse: (a) cross piece; (b) foot rest top — the dotted line indicates where this end is bevelled to fit snug against the rocker side panel; (c) foot rest support

Plate 19 Cutting out the plywood rocker panels using a jigsaw

side. The seat should, of course, fit snugly down onto the rockers, the tops of which, and the cross pieces, may need slight adjustment with plane or spokeshave to achieve this good fit. Don't fix the seat on permanently yet until the rump piece and seat back have been cut and fixed. But you can temporarily screw it in place while you plane the side edges level with the side panels. The rump piece is 2in (50mm) thick timber (I used jelutong) cut out and sanded smooth. The rear end of the rump piece is fixed level with the rear edge of the seat. You may like to bevel the front and edges of the seat so that it marries in nicely with the curves of the side panels. Two screws, and glue, are used to fix the rump piece in position. Make sure it is central on the seat panel.

The seat back is made by gluing two pieces of 3/8in (10mm) plywood together then cutting out the seat back shape from the resulting double thickness of plywood. (Alternatively, a piece of 3/4in (18mm) blockboard can be used.) The bottom edge of the seat back is carefully planed to a bevel so that it sits neatly against the rump piece and on the seat. When this has been done, pencil round the seat back

Plate 20 (above) Planing off the bevel of the batten to which the seat will be screwed. Note the blockboard cross piece on the bench

Plate 21 (below) Assembling the rockers with PVA glue and screws. Note that the battens and straight rocker top edges have been planed to form a bevel which allows the seat to sit snugly in place

on the seat (after ensuring it is centrally placed) and mark and drill for the screw holes. These are drilled and countersunk — two screws to come up through the seat into the back rest, one through the seat back into the rump piece — and all pieces glued and screwed together.

The foot rests (Plate 22) are cut from scraps of 1in x 3in (25mm x 75mm) solid wood and should be shaped to fit snugly to the side panels. A single screw holds the two parts of the foot rest together, while three screws (not forgetting glue as well) hold each foot rest onto the side panel, screwed from the inside.

The screw holes should now be filled, and if you are intending to varnish the rocking-horse choose a filler which matches the wood colour. Then it can be given a final thorough sanding down and is finished, except for the head.

The 'Mark 1' Cut-out Head (Fig 7)
This is the simplest head, cut from 1½in (38mm) thick timber. I used a piece of jelutong, but other woods would do just as well, if not better, since jelutong is not a particularly attractive wood for a varnished and polished finish, though it does blend in well with the birch plywood rockers. After the pattern has been marked on the wood it can be cut out quite easily by hand with a coping saw

Plate 22 Detail of foot rest. The two parts of the foot rest have been glued and screwed together with a single screw from the top (which has been filled). The foot rest has then been glued and screwed in position with three screws from the inside of the rockers

Plate 23 The completed rocking-horse with the 'Mark 1' head

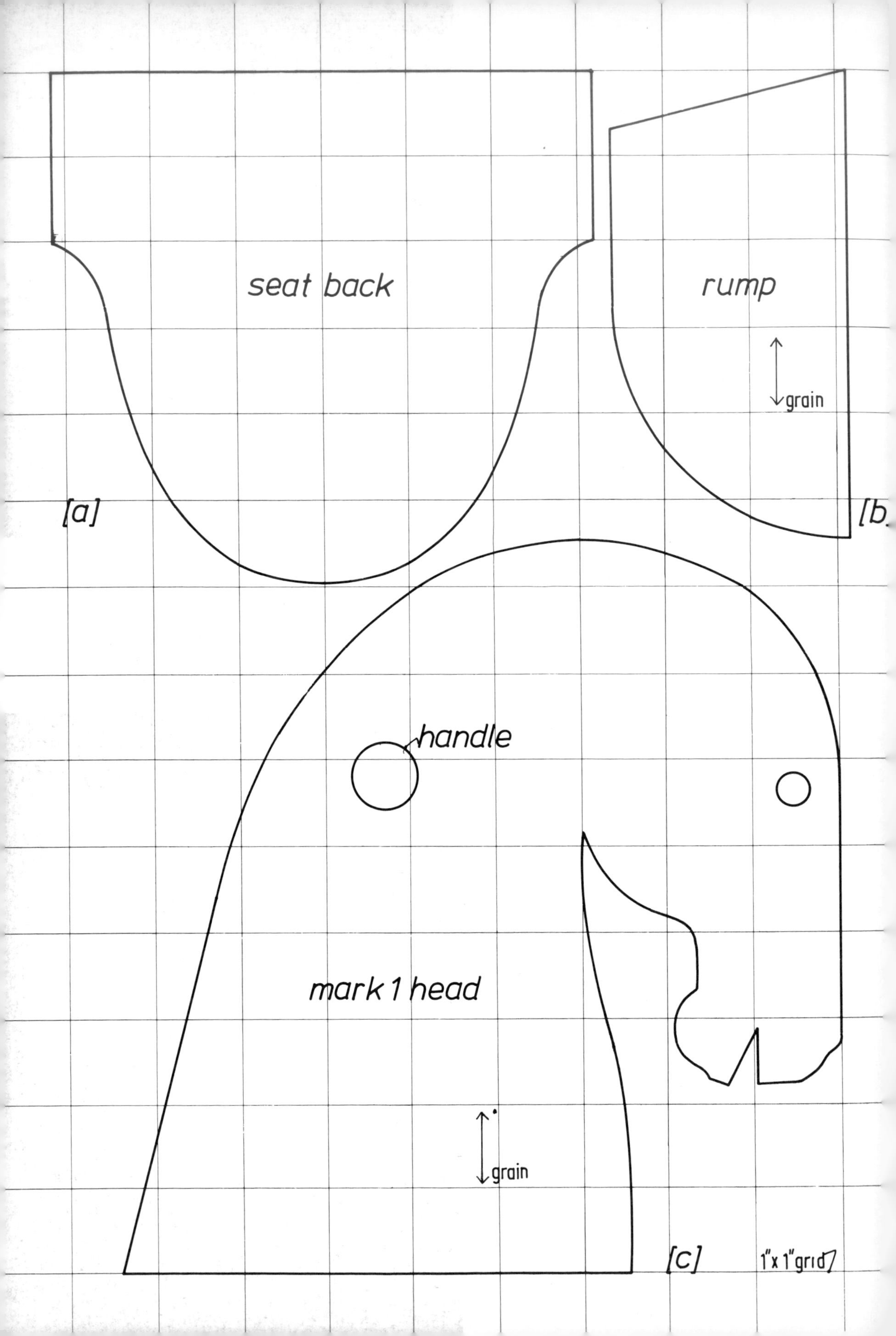
seat back
[a]
rump
grain
[b]
handle
mark 1 head
grain
[c]
1"x 1"grid

and, apart from sanding smooth, is not shaped any further. The eyes are 3⁄8in (10mm) holes drilled just a little way into the wood. The handle is made from a length of 3⁄4in (19mm) dowel set centrally in a hole drilled right through the neck and glued in place. Make sure that the bottom edge of the neck fits snugly down onto the seat in the middle, and mark for two screw holes, then glue and screw the head in position (Plate 23). Varnish or paint as desired.

The 'Mark 2' Simple Carved Head (Fig 8)
The second head is carved to a degree, so two or three chisels are needed. A few carving gouges will be handy here and also a sharp penknife can be usefully employed. (More information about tackling carving is given in Chapter 4.) The head and neck are cut in one piece from 2in (50mm) thick jelutong; the two neck muscle blocks, cut with the coping saw from 1in (25mm) thick jelutong are glued at either side (Plate 24). The bottom of the neck is planed quite flat so that it sits well on the seat top. To assist in holding the head in the vice while it is being worked, a block of scrap wood is screwed onto the underside of the neck (Plate 25). The bottom of the neck, where it sits on the seat, will wind up egg-shaped when viewed from underneath — this shape is shown in Fig 8 and can be drawn onto the underside of the neck to assist in cutting away the wood evenly at each side.

Starting from the base of the neck, chisel away the wood to achieve the upward taper of the neck rounded off over the top and back. The approximate shapes and positions of the ears, eyes, cheeks and nostrils are roughly sketched in pencil onto the wood of the head before carving. The head tapers somewhat towards the mouth, which is rounded off, but the 'eyebrows' and nostrils are left proud. The ears are separated with a coping saw and shaped with a small gouge or chisel. The eyes are lightly carved in relief and the mouth area cut away to suggest teeth (Plate 26). It is well for the inexperienced carver to cut some wood away from one side of the head, turn the piece and cut away a similar amount on the other

Fig 7 Scale drawing of simple rocking-horse: (a) seat back; (b) rump piece; (c) the 'Mark 1' cut-out head with position of handle

Plate 24 The 'Mark 2' head showing the neck muscle blocks glued in place, ready for carving

Plate 25 The 'Mark 2' head: the shaping of the neck is almost complete and a few initial cuts have been made on the head. Note the piece of scrap wood screwed onto the bottom of the neck so the head can be easily held in a vice

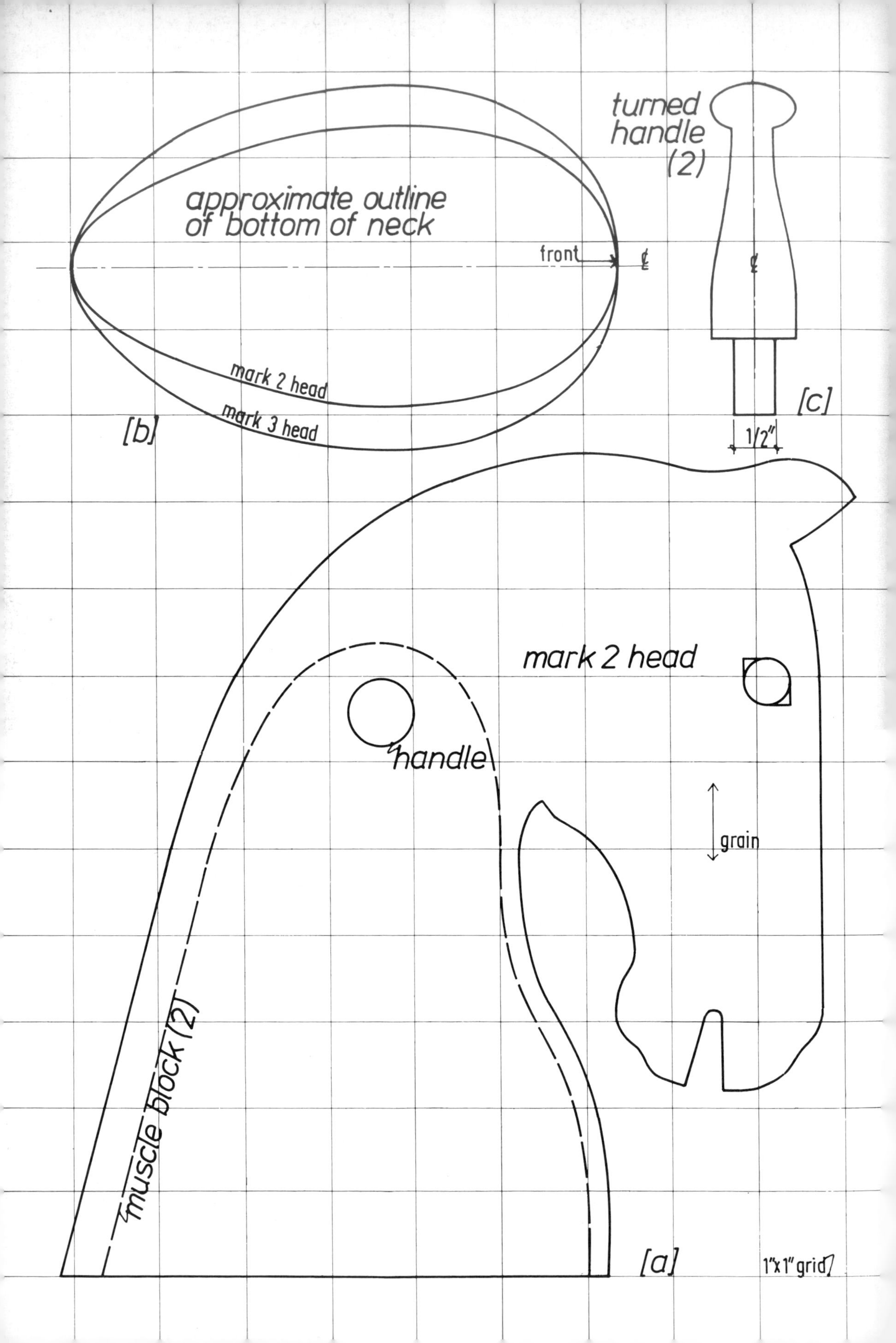

approximate outline
of bottom of neck
front
℄
mark 2 head
mark 3 head
[b]
turned
handle
(2)
℄
[c]
1/2"
mark 2 head
handle
grain
muscle block (2)
[a]
1"x1" grid

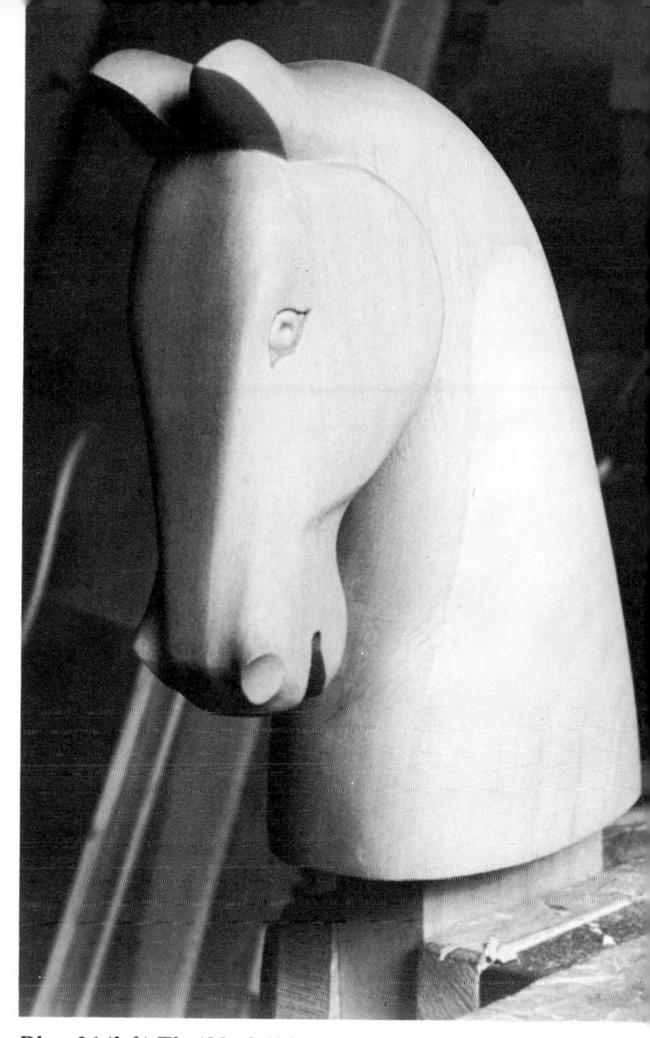

side to maintain the symmetry, then stand back and have a good look to see where more should be cut. Once the head and neck has been satisfactorily shaped and rounded it is given a thorough sanding down (Plate 27) ready for varnishing or painting, as preferred.

If handles are to be fitted these can be turned on a lathe from small offcuts of some suitable timber (as shown in Plate 28) or you can simply use a length of 3/4in (19mm) dowel glued into a hole drilled at right angles through the neck. The head is glued and screwed into position centrally on the front end of the seat, but this time use four screws to hold it firmly in place while the glue dries (Plate 29).

Fig 8 Scale drawing of simple rocking-horse: (a) the 'Mark 2' simple carved head with neck muscle block; (b) approximate outline of shape of the bottom of the neck where it joins onto the seat, for the 'Mark 2' and 'Mark 3' heads; (c) drawing of turned handle which may be fitted. A 3/4in (19mm) dia. dowel handle 8in (203mm) long right through the neck would also be quite satisfactory

Plate 26 (left) The 'Mark 2' head nearing completion

Plate 27 (right) The finished 'Mark 2' head: the ears have been 'separated' with a coping saw and the detail of the eyes cut in light relief

The 'Mark 3' Carved Head (Fig 9)

This head is more completely carved and in addition to the neck muscle blocks, in this case 1½in (38mm) thick jelutong glued either side of the neck, a small piece of wood ½in (13mm) thick is glued on each side in the area of the ears and eyes (Plate 31). These eye and ear pieces allow the ears to be set at a more realistic angle and allow the top of the forehead to be slightly broader, thus accentuating the taper of the head towards the mouth.

The procedure is similar to that in the 'Mark 2' but the head is worked more carefully and with a greater attention to detail. In particular, the muscling of the neck is suggested; the cheeks are shaped and less flat with a suggestion of the 'bone structure'; in the mouth the

Plate 28 The 'Mark 2' head showing the handles. These are turned on a lathe and glued in from either side — but a piece of dowel through the neck could well be used

Plate 29 The 'Mark 2' head mounted on the rockers

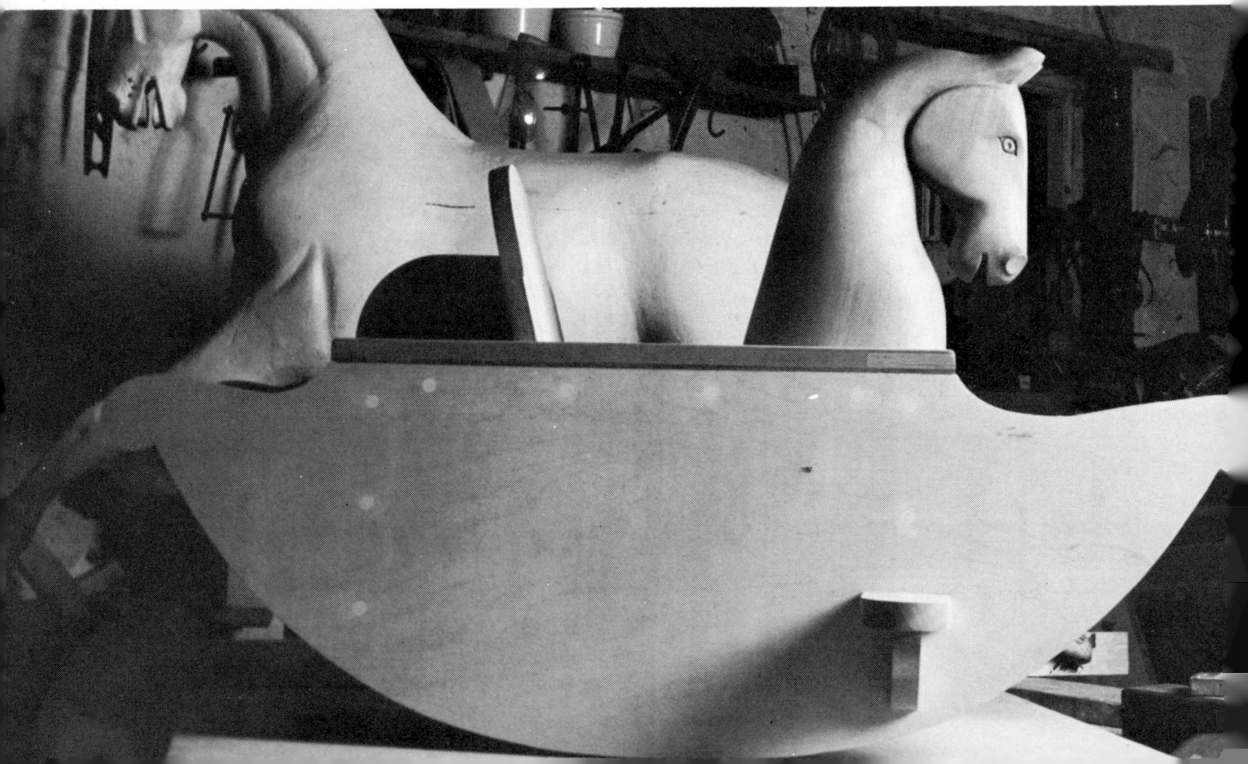

Plate 30 The completed rocking-horse with 'Mark 2' head; it is painted plain white and set off with touches of red to the ears, nostrils and mouth, and with a thin line painted in round the edges

teeth are shown top and bottom; the nostrils and ears are better shaped and slightly hollowed out (Plate 32).

If this sounds dreadfully complicated, I hope you will not be put off. A study of the accompanying photographs will give you an idea of what to aim for. In any case the horse's head shown here is a very long way from being like a real horse's head. A glance at the way the horses in St Mark's Square in Venice have been fashioned, or at any good classical equestrian statue for that matter, will demonstrate what can be achieved in creating a true likeness to the real thing. But that is hardly the point. After all, what you are trying to achieve here is a good, strong, workmanlike toy for children which is incidentally good to look at. The extent to which the maker takes pains over the details of the carving is for his or her personal satisfaction — children are unlikely to care much about it.

I fitted small glass eyes to this head (Plate 33) but you could just as well carve eyes into the wood in light relief and paint them. Glass eyes do have a charming glint in them — I never use plastic. Apart from that no other accessories were used since I deliberately wanted to keep the finishing uncomplicated, but a simple bridle and a padded seat could be fitted if desired. After the head is finished it is glued to the seat, being positioned centrally near the front and secured with glue and four screws (Plates 34 and 35). Finally the rocking-horse is varnished or painted, according to choice. Polyurethane varnish will give a hard tough coating; it goes on better if diluted slightly with white spirit (or turpentine). Three or four coats should be given, lightly sanding off with flour paper between coats. All paint should be of an approved low lead content. Two or three coats of gloss applied over a primer and a couple of undercoats will give a good finish (Plate 35).

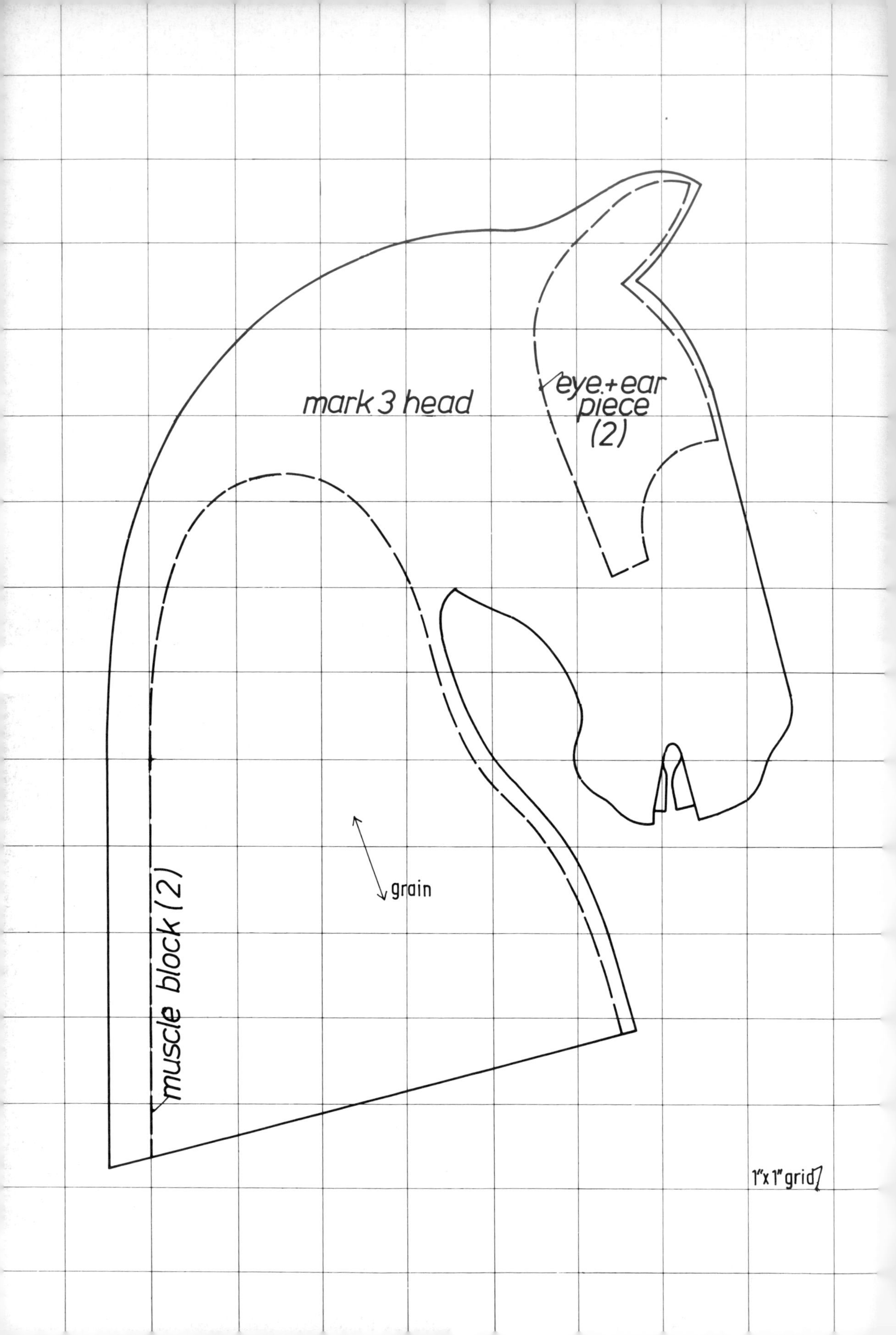
mark 3 head
eye+ear piece (2)
grain
muscle block (2)
1"x 1" grid

Plate 31 (above) The 'Mark 3' head with neck muscle blocks and ear/eye pieces glued in place ready for carving

Plate 32 (above right) The roughing out stage of the 'Mark 3' head carving

Plate 33 (right) The completed 'Mark 3' head fitted with glass eyes

Fig 9 Scale drawing of simple rocking-horse 'Mark 3' carved head with neck muscle block and eye and ear piece

Plate 34 'End on' view of the plywood rocking-horse fitted with the 'Mark 3' head

Plate 35 The complete rocking-horse with 'Mark 3' head, matt varnished and ready to ride

4
THE TRADITIONAL FULLY CARVED ROCKING-HORSE

The two rocking-horses in this section are designed for hand building and finishing in the traditional manner. There are various ways of building a wooden horse but the method described here is designed to be appropriate for the home hand craftsman with, probably, limited facilities. Details of two horses are given, a small model suitable for young children of about two to five years of age, and a larger model which can be ridden by much older children and even adults.

The construction method is broadly similar in the case of both horses though the small version is easier to build because it is lighter and requires less physical work — there is less waste wood to cut away. The main difference between the two rocking-horses lies in the mounting: the small model is mounted on curved bow rockers while the large is mounted on a swing iron stand (Plate 36). There are good reasons for this difference in mountings.

Bow shaped rockers look superb with their lovely sweep of timber, gently tapered, terminating in a rounded piece at each end, connected together with neatly turned cross pieces and the broader slatted platform in the middle. They allow an uncluttered view of the horse's legs outsplayed at full 'leap'. They give a lively and realistic ride and if they are properly constructed, that is, of sufficient length, the horse is immune from any tendency to tip over headlong. (This is important in a wooden horse, which may be quite heavy).

The bow shaped rockers on the small horse are designed to make the horse quite stable but, as mentioned in an earlier chapter, there are other drawbacks to this method of mounting. The bow rockers tend to move about on the floor when the horse is ridden, knocking into walls or scratching furniture that gets in the way, and perhaps crushing the toes of children standing too close. Also, a large horse requires very long bow rockers to maintain stability, consequently needing a large room to accommodate it. For these reasons I have confined the use of the bow rockers to the small horse while the larger horse is mounted on a steel swing iron safety stand. Horses mounted on bow rockers have their legs fixed so that they stretch further forward and back, allowing the hooves to be fixed near the extremities of the rockers. The legs of the stand mounted horse are more 'upright' giving it more of a prancing appearance.

The carving of the small horse shown is simpler and less detailed than that of the large version — but of course the carved finish depends upon the carver.

How to Tackle Carving

Building a fully carved rocking-horse involves carving 'in the round' and this presents special problems. The simpler heads described in the previous chapters are basically cut-out, silhouette shapes which look horse-like only when viewed from the side (except for the 'Mark 3' head of the simple plywood rocking-horse). By comparison, the fully carved horse needs to be given a horse-like appearance when viewed from all aspects and this is achieved by carving into the wooden blocks at different angles and depths. The carver needs to try to develop an eye for the three dimensions: to bear in mind always that a cut in from one side will inevitably alter the appearance of the carving when viewed from another angle. One's first attempts at carving in the round will be a continual process of trial and error and compromise; of frequently turning the work to get a different perspective on it. Details of the carving method for each of the parts of the horse will be given under the appropriate headings, but the following are a few general comments about how to approach carving.

The novice carver is likely to make either (or both) of two basic errors: carving away too much, or carving away too little. It is a maxim

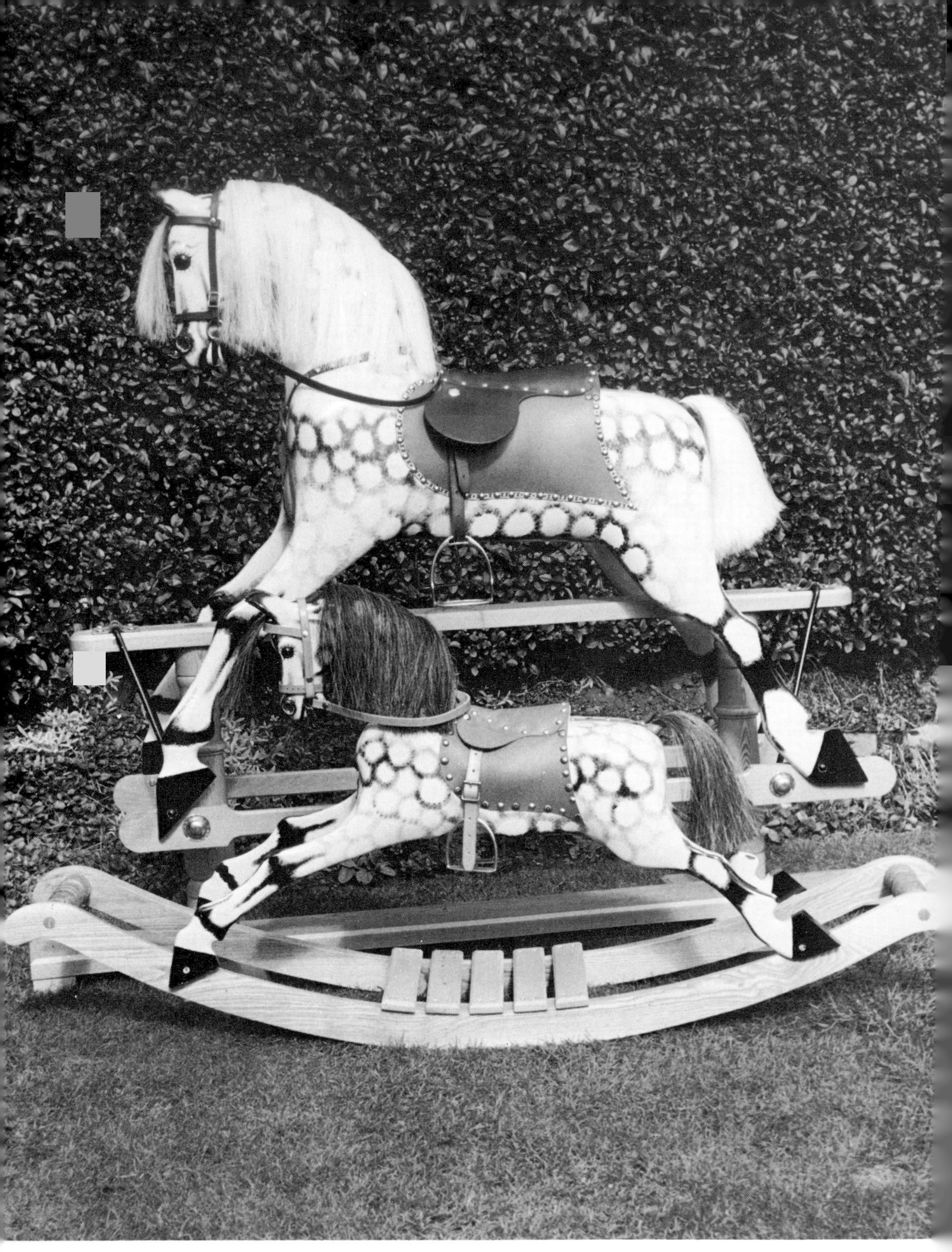

Plate 36 The complete large and small fully carved rocking-horses

of carving that once wood has been removed it cannot be replaced. If you find you have carved away too much in a particular area it is possible to splice in a fresh piece of wood and try again. But this is complicated and time consuming and should be avoided if possible, in accordance with another old woodworking maxim: think twice, cut once. Work over each side of the carving in turn, cutting away modest amounts of wood. Spend, say, ten minutes carving into one side of the horse, then turn the work or move round it and carve a corresponding amount of wood from the other side, aiming to keep the two sides symmetrical. Then stand back and see how it looks before returning to the first side and carving away some more.

Failing to carve away enough is almost as bad an error as carving away too much. Prior to your commencing the carving, the body is essentially a rectangular box. But by the time the carving is complete virtually all trace of that ugly square 'boxiness' should have disappeared, to be replaced by lovely flowing arcs and curves.

On the whole, wood carvers who produce successful results have a very clear idea in their heads of what they are going to do before picking up the mallet and gouge. This means planning in advance. This book contains a lot of photographs and drawings which I hope will help you in forming a good idea of the rocking-horse, but there is no substitute for actually doing it. Ultimately you will be alone with your gouge and your mallet and your blocks of wood. You are about to set off upon one of the most exciting adventures, to create, from a pile of rough and dirty timber, a lovely thing. On the other hand, if you are not sure about where you are going to cut, you may only be setting off to make firewood. So how can you ensure that your carving will be successful? You cannot guarantee it. Every shift of the gouge, every blow of the mallet will involve some risks, but these risks are a vital part of the ultimate satisfaction to be gained from the project. A good plan is to study each part of the horse carefully before the carving starts, and to make models in clay or Plasticine. This will give you a fair idea of the shapes involved and of course it is far easier to correct errors made in a Plasticine model than in a carving.

It is necessary to have some means of holding the horse while it is being worked upon. I know of one rocking-horse maker who regularly uses a 'Workmate' to hold his rocking-horses and who says it is an ideal portable vice. I have a very heavy old bench and an ancient cast iron vice which can hold anything immobile. The problem with bench vices is that you are continually working low down near the bench top so that the bench itself often obstructs the use of your tools on the work, or the rocking-horse's legs become fouled up with the sides and legs of the bench. The best holding device for carving is the carver's chops. This is essentially a wooden vice which clamps (with a screw and wing nut) onto the bench top. It can be moved around to suit the required position of the work and, since the jaws are narrow, it hardly obstructs the use of the tools at all. Also the work is higher up, at a level where I find it more comfortable to work (but perhaps that's just because I'm rather tall and my bench top is too low). The carver's chops which can be seen in Plate 58 on page 69 are made from an old vice screw and some hardwood offcuts, but they can be purchased from good tools suppliers who specialise in carver's equipment (see Appendix 3).

Handtools

4 (preferably 6) sash or sliding cramps, minimum capacity 18in (450mm)
4 x 8in (200mm) G cramps
Jack or fore plane
Cross-cut saw
Coping saw
Hand or electric drill with ¼in (6mm) and ½in (13mm) twist drills
Brace with ¾in (19mm), 1in (25mm) and 1⅜in (35mm) twist bits
Bevel-edge chisels: ¼in (6mm), ½in (13mm) and 1in (25mm)
Gouges: ¼in (6mm), ½in (13mm) and 1in (25mm)
Carver's mallet
Flat face spokeshave
Drawknife
Round and curved surforms
Glass or garnet paper in fine and coarse grades

The chisels and gouges listed above are really the minimum required. If you haven't tackled

Plate 37 A selection of carving tools. Top, left to right: spokeshave, drawknife, spokeshave (curved sole type). Bottom, left to right: small straight deep gouge; 3/8in (10mm) bent gouge, 1in (25mm) straight gouge, 1in (25mm) spade gouge, 3/8in (10mm) skew end chisel, 1 1/4in (32mm) firmer chisel, beech carver's mallet, 1 1/4in (32mm) straight gouge, 1/2in (13mm) gouge, 1in (25mm) shallow gouge, 5/8in (16mm) deep gouge, 5/8in (16mm) salmon bend gouge, 5/16in (8mm) bevel-edge firmer chisel

any carving before it is probably not a bad idea to buy one of the sets of carving gouges that are to be found in any hardware store. The trouble with these sets, however, is that they always seem to include one or two tools that you will never use. Also, for a large piece of carving like a rocking-horse you will need at least one or two large gouges and these are almost never included in the sets. Once you start on the carving you will almost certainly get to a point where you will feel a definite need for a particular size or shape of gouge and it is at this point that you should go out and buy that gouge. If you do not live close to a good supplier of carving tools, there are several firms dealing in tools by post who carry a good choice of chisels and gouges which can be ordered individually, though these may cost rather more than buying them 'off the shelf' (see Appendix 3).

It is essential to have a decent, fairly heavy, woodcarver's mallet; that is, one with a round head, made of beech or lignum vitae, with an ash handle.

The drawknife is very useful though not vital. It will take a little practice to get the hang of its effective use, but will enable you to cut away wood accurately and quickly during the roughing out of the rocking-horse shape.

In addition to the coping saw listed, I have a 15in (380mm) bow saw which I find useful for literally cutting corners.

The round surform is particularly useful for getting at some of the more awkward curves, such as the front of the neck under the 'chin'. Surforms can shift soft wood quite quickly and are easy to use and control, the main problem with the round one being that it gets clogged up with shavings inside, which have to be shaken out periodically.

A good quality resin glue, such as Cascamite, should be used throughout.

Power Tools

It is possible to build these rocking-horses entirely by hand, without employing any machines at all. A person with sufficient stamina could hand work all the parts even for the larger horse. However, without detracting from the essentially hand-built qualities of the finished article, some power tools can be usefully employed, especially in the cutting out of the various parts. A jigsaw can be used to cut out the legs and muscle blocks, though a band-saw is better. A band-saw is really essential for cutting out the shape of the head and neck. You will probably want to order your timber from the merchant ready planed. A timber merchant who has a joinery department, or a local joiner, can often be persuaded, at a modest cost, to cut out the parts of the head, neck, legs etc on his band-saw, if you draw out the patterns for him on the timber.

A hand power drill and ½in (13mm) flat bit will enable you to drill the holes for the dowel pegs quickly and an orbital finishing sander is useful on the stand. A disc sander attachment on the electric drill can be used for sanding off the body of the horse, though this has to be used carefully as it tends to be rather fierce. The top edges of the stand are chamfered and a router with chamfering cutter will speed up this process though it is easy enough to do by hand with a plane. A hand-held electric planer can be useful in quickly shaping wood during the roughing-out stage, though personally I find a big gouge and mallet just as fast, and far more easily controlled.

The stand posts and (on the small horse) the rocker end pieces are turned on a lathe. In the absence of a lathe, however, these parts can be made of rectangular or square section timber, the ends cut to appropriate sized tenons to be morticed into the stand or rockers, rather than turned down to an appropriate diameter to peg into a round hole, as is the case when using the lathe. Again, it may be possible to find someone who will turn these items for you without charging the earth.

Types of Timber

Over many years various timbers, hard and soft, have been employed in rocking-horse making. The commonest timbers used on the traditional Victorian rocking-horse were yellow pine for the head and body, beech for the legs. Stands were made of almost anything, particularly if they were to be painted over, when two or even three different woods might be used, presumably whatever was available at the time. Stand posts were often of elm or beech, sometimes oak. The rest of the stand might be of oak but more commonly of pine (yellow, redwood or paraná). I currently use Douglas fir to make all my stands. On good horses, bow shaped rockers are almost invariably of ash.

The timber chosen for the body and the head of the horse should be one which is fairly easy to work and is stable, that is, once it is assembled it stays put and does not tend to warp and open up cracks. Few experiences can be more disheartening than to have spent a good deal of time and effort building a horse only to find gaping cracks opening up as the timber moves. Yellow pine is easily workable and stable (as evidenced by the fact that for many years it was the favoured timber of pattern makers) but these days has become difficult to obtain and more expensive. An excellent alternative is jelutong from Malaya (used by many of those pattern makers who still employ timber). It is a lovely carving wood, close grained, knot-free, easy to work and very stable. Its major fault is that its surface is marred by latex ducts — small oval holes up to ⅝in (16mm) or so long, which run right through the wood across the grain. Jelutong is also not an attractive wood; it is pale yellow and lacks pleasing grain patterning or figure. But since in this case the wood will ultimately be painted over, the latex ducts can be filled as the surface of the wood is hidden. Some people like a natural wood finish; if you think you might like to varnish the completed horse rather than paint it in the traditional manner, a wood with a more attractive grain pattern should be chosen. Take the advice of your timber merchant on this; your final choice of timber will inevitably be something of a compromise between what you want and what your timber merchant can supply.

It is important that all timber used in the building of the rocking-horse should be well seasoned. The old rocking-horse makers would, after assembling and rough carving the horse from air-seasoned stock, put the rocking-horse 'on the shelf' for six or nine months for a thorough drying out, after which time the finishing carving was done and any blemishes or cracks filled in. These days few people are likely to have that much patience, so it is well worth while paying the extra cost for kiln-dried timber. In this way you can ensure the dryness of your timber and be reasonably certain that, providing your horse has been worked upon in dry conditions throughout, when it is eventually taken into a centrally heated room, the timber will remain 'unmoved'.

Making the Horse

Cutting Lists

Thicknesses given in the following cutting lists are nominal, ie 3in (75mm) thick nominal will finish, after planing, at 2¾in (71mm). Widths and lengths are those actually required, allowing for minimum wastage — but are subject to adjustment. For example, if, for the legs of the large horse, you find you are unable to obtain a beech board 9in (230mm) wide, then a 7in (180mm) wide board will do, but will have to be much longer — ie 100in (2,540mm) — because the leg patterns will not now overlap so much. Similarly with the other parts, by shuffling the patterns around all pieces of similar thickness, and sometimes using offcuts of other timber, a most judicious and economical selection of timber can be made.

Cutting List — Large Fully Carved Rocking-horse

	Thickness x Width x Length	*Wood*
Head	3 x 7 x 12in (75 x 178 x 305mm)	Jelutong
Eye and ear pieces	½ x 4 x 12in (12 x 100 x 305mm)	Jelutong
Neck	3 x 10 x 19in (75 x 254 x 483mm)	Jelutong
1st neck muscle blocks	1½ x 10 x 16in (38 x 254 x 406mm)	Jelutong
2nd neck muscle blocks	1½ x 9 x 8in (38 x 229 x 203mm)	Jelutong
Upper body block	3 x 10 x 27½in (75 x 254 x 698mm)	Jelutong
Lower body block	3 x 10 x 27½in (75 x 254 x 698mm)	Jelutong
Middle body blocks (sides) x 2	3 x 4 x 27½in (75 x 100 x 698mm)	Jelutong
Middle body blocks (ends) x 2	3 x 4 x 5in (75 x 100 x 127mm)	Jelutong
Leg muscle blocks	1 x 7 x 38in (25 x 178 x 965mm)	Jelutong
Legs	1½ x 9 x 72in (38 x 230 x 1,830mm)	Beech
Cross struts x 2	1 x 3 x 49in (25 x 75 x 1,245mm)	Beech
Pegs	½in(dia.) x 36in (12 x 914mm)	Dowel

	Stand	
Top	1 x 4 x 52in (25 x 100 x 1,320mm)	Douglas fir
Bottom	1½ x 6 x 60in (38 x 150 x 1,524mm)	Douglas fir
Cross pieces x 2	1½ x 6 x 21in (38 x 150 x 535mm)	Douglas fir
End pieces x 2	1½ x 3 x 5½in (38 x 75 x 140mm)	Douglas fir
Stand posts x 2	4 x 4 x 24in (100 x 100 x 610mm)	Douglas fir
Saddle block	1 x 3 x 8in (25 x 75 x 205mm)	Douglas fir

Cutting List — Small Fully Carved Rocking-horse

	Thickness x Width x Length	*Wood*
Head	2 x 6 x 8in (50 x 150 x 203mm)	Jelutong
Eye and ear pieces	½ x 1½ x 10in (12 x 38 x 254mm)	Jelutong
Neck	2 x 7 x 12in (50 x 178 x 305mm)	Jelutong
Neck muscle blocks	1½ x 6 x 17in (38 x 150 x 432mm)	Jelutong
Upper body block	2 x 7 x 18in (50 x 178 x 457mm)	Jelutong
Lower body block	3 x 7 x 18in (75 x 178 x 457mm)	Jelutong
Middle body blocks (sides) x 2	2 x 2 x 18in (50 x 50 x 457mm)	Jelutong
Middle body blocks (ends) x 2	2 x 2 x 4½in (50 x 50 x 115mm)	Jelutong
Leg muscle blocks	1 x 6 x 27in (25 x 150 x 690mm)	Jelutong
Legs	1 x 6 x 55in (25 x 150 x 1,400mm)	Beech

Rockers	1 x 12 x 60in (25 x 305 x 1,525mm)	Ash
End pieces x 2	2 x 2 x 11in (50 x 50 x 280mm)	Ash
Pegs	½in(dia.) x 24in (12 x 610mm)	Dowel

The following parts are cut from the remaining ash after the curved rockers have been cut out.

Slatted platform x 5	¾ x 2 x 11½in (18 x 50 x 292mm)
Frame side pieces x 2	1 x 3 x 12in (25 x 75 x 305mm)
Frame end pieces x 2	1 x 2 x 12in (25 x 50 x 305mm)
Saddle block	1 x 2 x 5in (25 x 50 x 130mm)

The head, neck, muscle blocks (neck and leg) and legs should be drawn out full size to be used as patterns. The scale plans may be transferred onto squared paper or card, or ready drawn full sized patterns can be obtained (see Appendix 3).

The patterns are cut out and pinned onto the timber and drawn round (Figs 10, 11 and 12). The shapes can then be sawn out and this is facilitated by drilling a number of ½in or ¾in (13mm or 19mm) holes at places where the saw blade has to take an awkward sharp turn, eg under the chin. Where the plan shows cramping noggins, care should be taken to leave these in place since they will greatly ease cramping together of the parts during assembly. The remainder of the parts — the upper, middle and lower body blocks — are cross cut from the boards. No shaping is done on these prior to assembly. The order for assembly of the parts of the horse is briefly as follows:

1 Head to neck (plus eye and ear pieces).
2 Neck to upper body block.
3 Neck muscle blocks to neck.
4 Legs to lower body block.
5 Leg muscle blocks to legs.
6 Middle body blocks to lower body block.
7 Upper body block to middle body block.

Do not worry unduly about great precision when placing the blocks together. There will be ample overlap between each (as shown in the photographs), which will be carved away.

The instructions refer to both the large and the small horses, except where the difference is specifically mentioned.

The Head and Neck

It will be noted that the head lies at an angle of 15° or so to the side, left or right, it doesn't matter which. This angle is enhanced in the case of the large horse (see Fig 11), whose head and neck are cut from separate blocks, by leaving an allowance of an extra ½in (13mm) or so on the head, which is bevelled before the head is glued to the neck. Later, when the neck is fitted down onto the upper body block, the neck will be further angled to the line of the body. This angling of the head lends the horse a touch of 'life', an impression of it just tossing its head a little, which is lacking in horses whose heads are fixed in a stiff straight line with the body. The effect is well worth the slight extra effort. The head is glued to the neck using a sash cramp on the cramping noggin on the neck, the waste piece cut from the front of the head and a wedge or two of scrap wood (Plate 38). If, prior to gluing up, you half tap in to the middle of the area to be glued a couple of 1in (25mm) panel pins, and nip their heads off, these will stop the two parts sliding about when the cramp is tightened. In this, and in all the glued joints on the horse, care should be taken to make sure the joint is good — that the surfaces come together over the whole of the glued area, which should

Fig 10 Scale drawing of parts of the small fully-carved rocking-horse

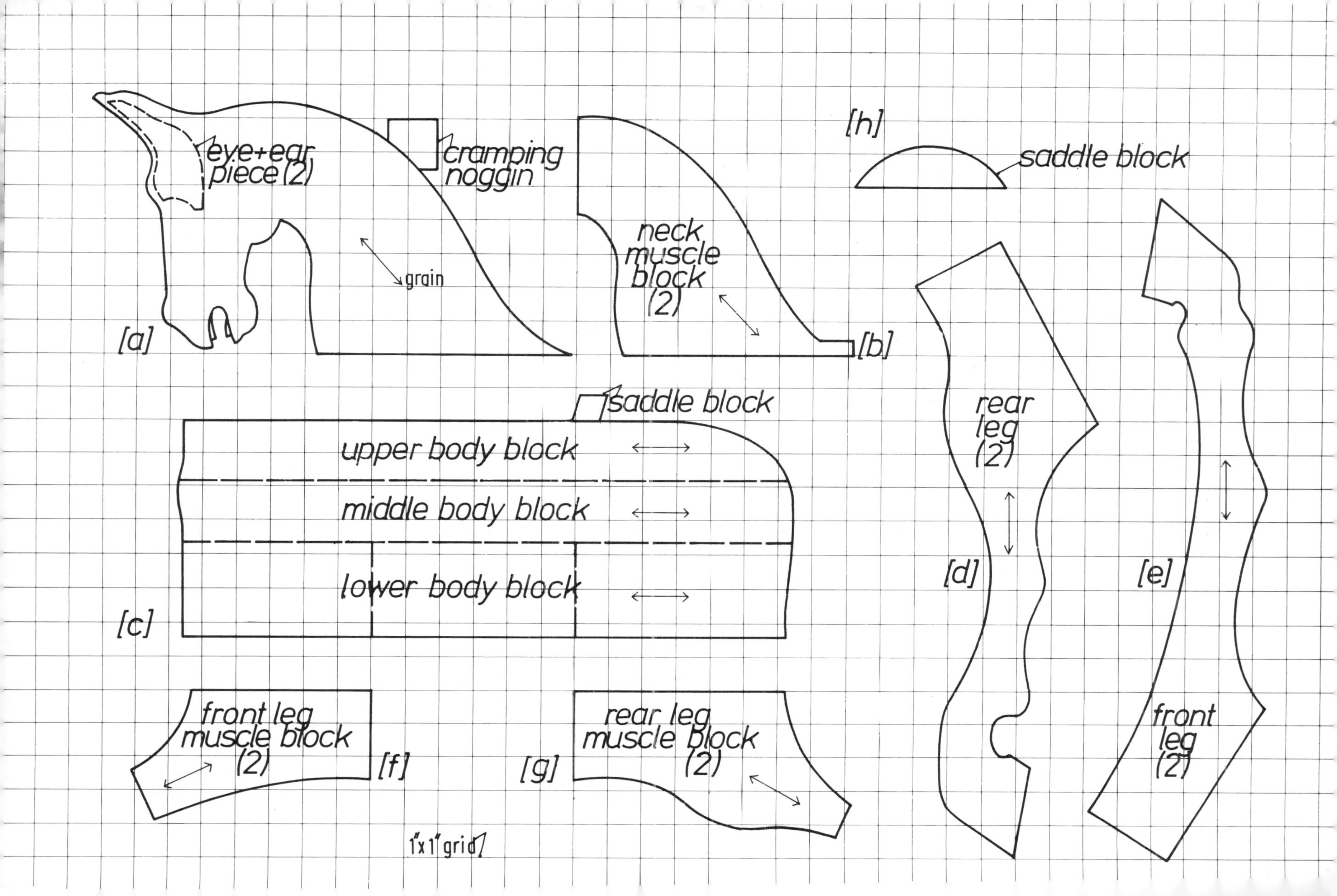
eye+ear piece (2)
cramping noggin
grain
[a]
neck muscle block (2)
[b]
[h]
saddle block
saddle block
upper body block
middle body block
lower body block
[c]
rear leg (2)
[d]
front leg (2)
[e]
front leg muscle block (2)
[f]
rear leg muscle block (2)
[g]
1"x1" grid

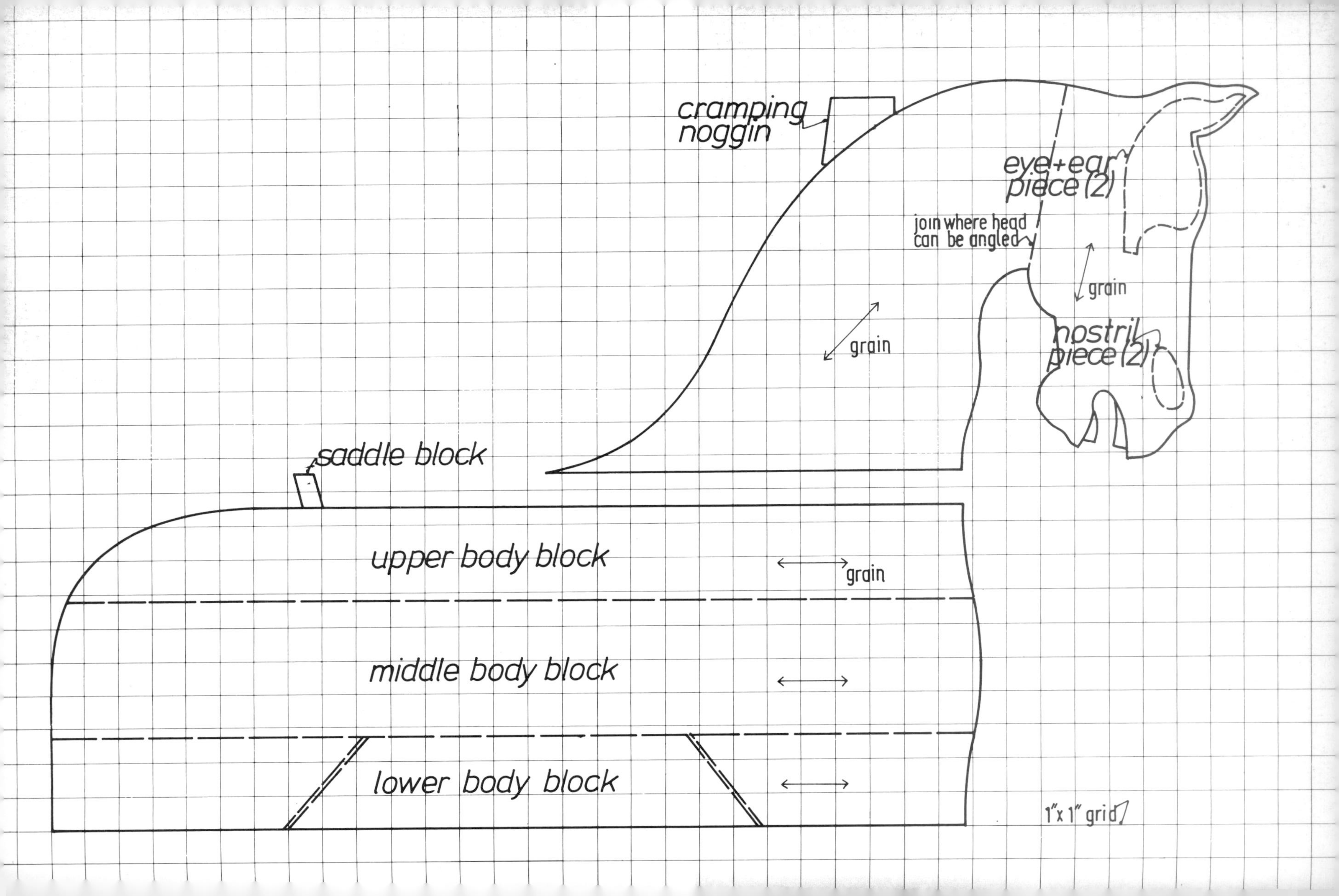
cramping noggin
eye+ear piece (2)
join where head can be angled
grain
grain
nostril piece (2)
saddle block
upper body block
grain
middle body block
lower body block
1"x 1" grid

be roughened slightly to help the glue to penetrate the pores in the wood. The small blocks which broaden the head at the eyes and ears are glued in place (Plate 39) and held with a G cramp. After the head and neck are fixed together I normally do most of the carving of the detail of the head before fixing it to the body. It is much easier to move around like this. As the head of the horse tends to be the focus of attention it is worth taking special care with the carving.

Use the 1in (25mm) chisel first, to give it the slight taper towards the mouth. Then the details of the cheeks, the exaggerated flare of the nostrils, the eyes, and jaws are roughed out using progressively smaller chisels and gouges to form the curves (Plates 40 and 41). Approximate outlines of the proposed cuts should be pencilled in before you start cutting into the wood, to ensure that, for example, the eyes and nostrils are at the same level at each side. The ears are separated first with a coping saw, then carved into shape (Plate 42). The insides of the ears and nostrils are hollowed out (Plate

Fig 11 Scale drawing of large fully-carved rocking-horse head, neck and body blocks

Plate 38 Large horse: gluing up the head to the neck
Plate 39 Large horse head: eye, ear and nostril pieces glued in place, ready for carving to commence

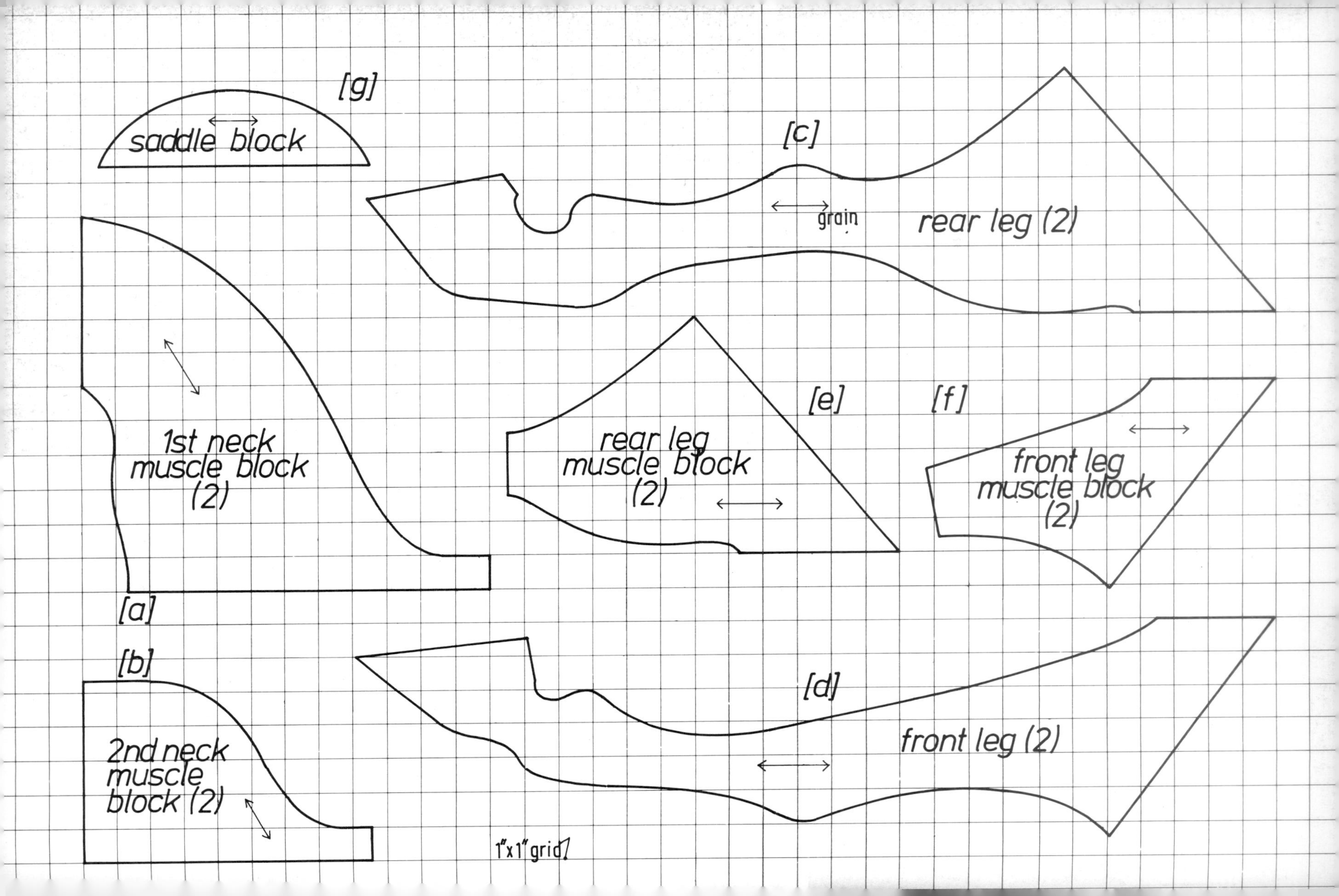
[g]
saddle block
[c]
grain
rear leg (2)
1st neck muscle block (2)
[a]
rear leg muscle block (2)
[e]
[f]
front leg muscle block (2)
[b]
2nd neck muscle block (2)
[d]
front leg (2)
1"x1" grid

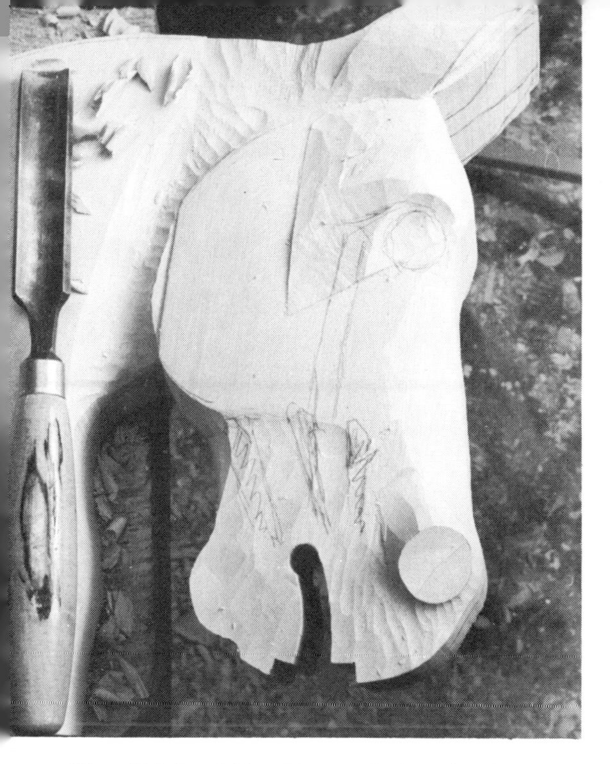

Plate 40 (above) Roughing out the large head. Approximate positions of the features have been pencilled in; the first cuts are made with a 1in (25mm) firmer chisel and the 1in (25mm) gouge shown

Plate 41 (above right) The roughing out stage is nearly complete. Smaller gouges have been used to cut out the eye recesses and clean up the detail of the features. The salmon bend gouge shown is useful for 'scooping' out under the cheeks

Plate 42 (right) Separating the ears with a coping saw

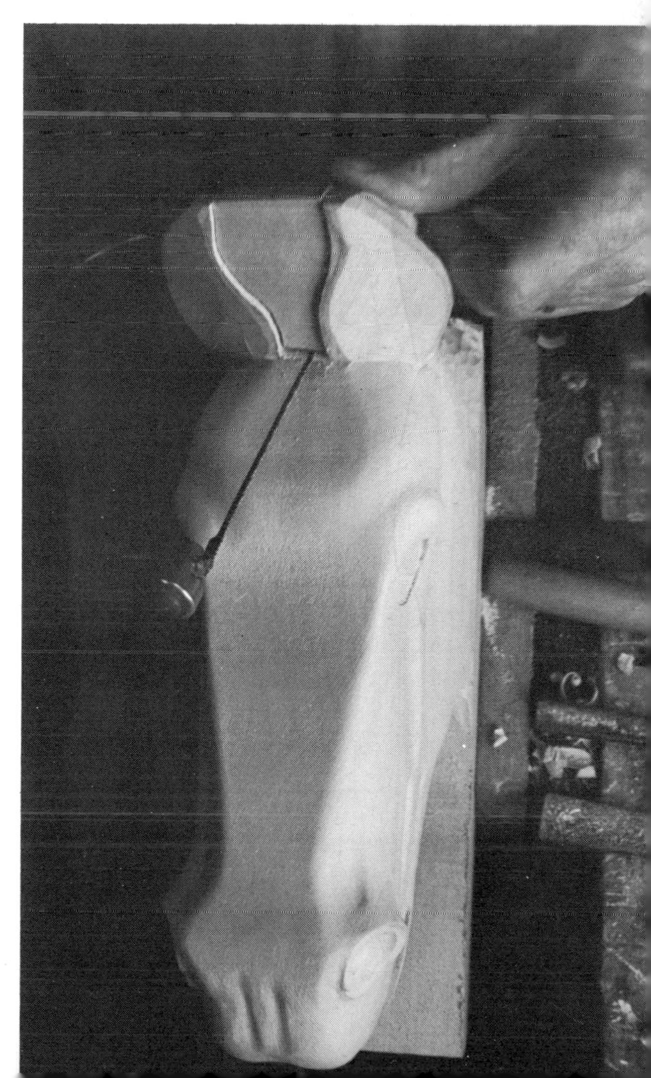

43) only slightly to avoid leaving very thin and fragile edges and it is important to leave the base of the ears, where they join the top of the head, fairly broad for extra strength. The recesses which will later take the glass eyes are round, about 3/16in (4mm) deep and 7/8in (21mm) diameter (large horse) and 5/8in (16mm) diameter (small horse). The head is finished off with fine glasspaper (Plates 44 and 45).

The neck and head can now be glued down onto the upper body block, as mentioned above, angling the neck to the line of the body. A piece of scrap wood about 10in (255mm) long is nailed across the top of the cramping noggin on the large neck and a sash cramp at

Fig 12 Scale drawing of large fully-carved horse legs, and neck and leg muscle blocks

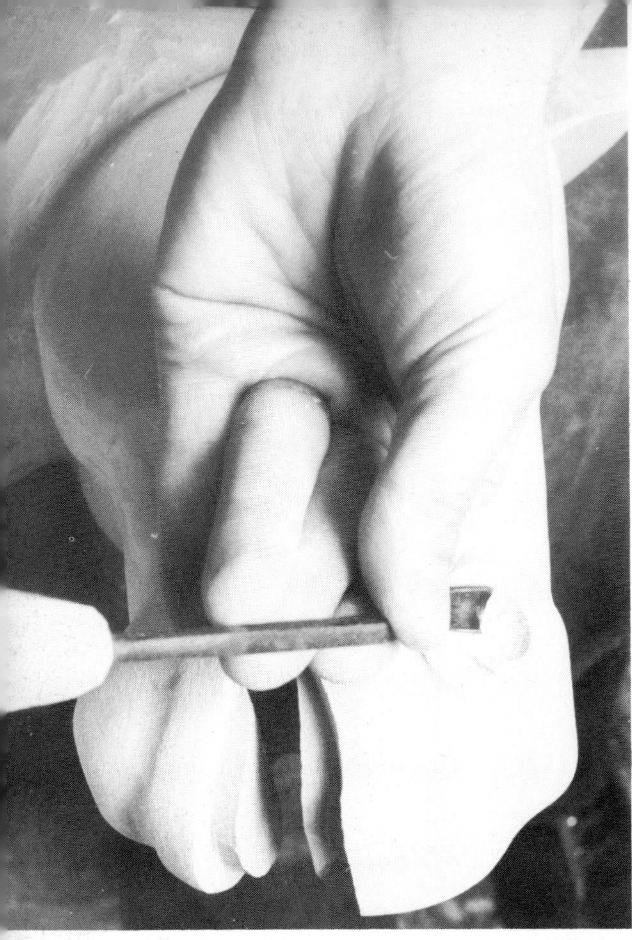

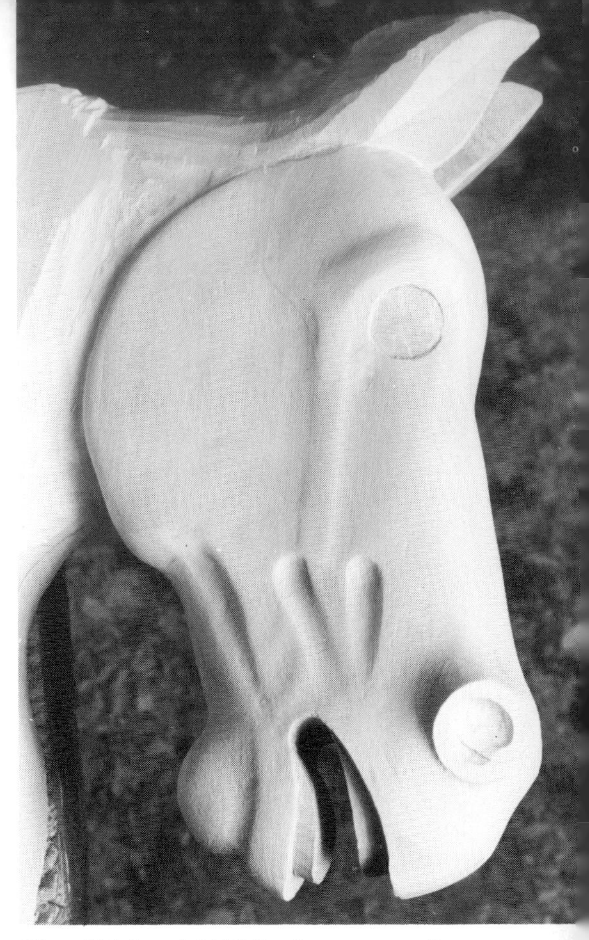

Plate 43 (above left) Hollowing out a nostril

Plate 44 (above) Large horse head carving nearing completion

Plate 45 (left) The large head carving complete and ready for the eyes to be fitted. It has been smoothed over with medium grit garnet paper

Plate 46 (opposite top left) Small horse: the head, showing ear and eye pieces glued on ready for carving to commence

Plate 47 (opposite top right) Roughing out

Plate 48 (opposite bottom left) The small horse head, showing the taper of the head towards the mouth. The ears have been separated with a coping saw

Plate 49 (opposite bottom right) The carving virtually complete; the head has been sanded down and the glass eyes fitted

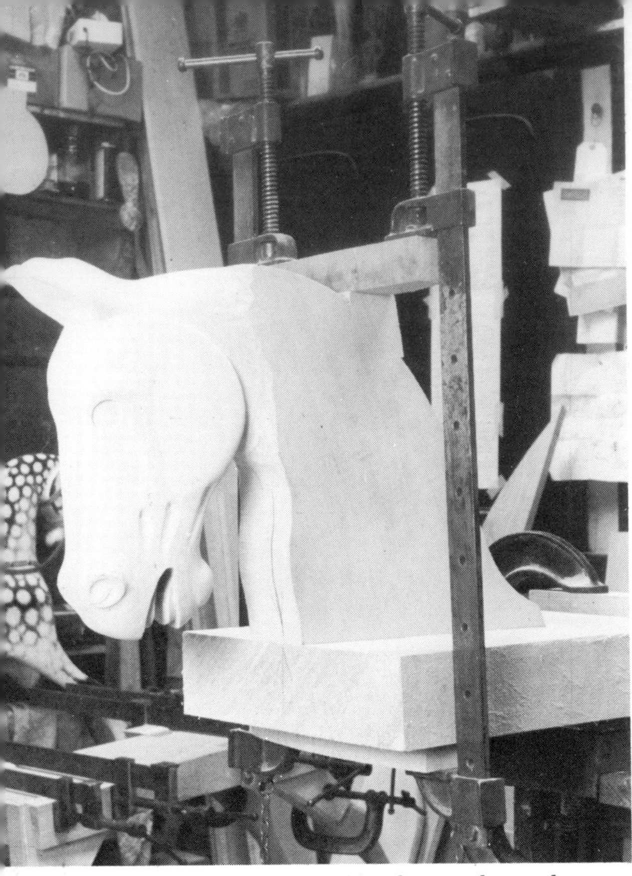

Plate 50 Cramping the large horse neck onto the upper body block

each side employed to cramp the neck firmly down (Plate 50). The head and neck of the small horse can be held in place with a single deep-throated sliding cramp. The neck muscle blocks are planed to fit snugly onto the sides of the neck and upper body block and glued and cramped in place. The secure fixing of the neck is assisted by pegging through from the underside of the upper body block into the neck and neck muscle blocks. The pegs are of ½in (13mm) diameter dowelling and are fixed after the neck and neck muscle blocks have been glued in place. If ordinary round dowelling is used, a shaving planed off along the dowel will allow surplus glue to escape. Drill ½in (13mm) holes and drive the pegs in (plus glue) with a hammer. The ends are then trimmed off flush with the surface with a saw and paring chisel. All this takes a little time, and while you are waiting for the glue to dry you can turn your attention to the lower extremities.

Legs and Body

As with the head, it is easier to carve the lower parts of the legs before fixing them. From the knees down to the hooves they are rounded off and the hocks are narrowed slightly. A surform and spokeshave are useful for this operation.

The legs join into the large body at an angle which gives them the characteristic splay (Fig 13). The angle of the splay is approximately 10° when viewed from above and 10° when viewed from the front or back. If this is not done the horse can end up looking oddly knock-kneed. These angles are cut into the lower body block and the legs butt jointed onto the sides (Plate 51). The legs of the small horse are simpler — splaying at about 10° when viewed from above (Fig 14) they do not have the combined angling of the large horse's legs. Many old rocking-horses have the legs morticed into the body and of course this is perfectly satisfactory, but it is probably easier for the handworker to butt joint them as described here, and, given good modern glues, stronger too. The wedge-shaped scrap pieces which have been cut from each corner of the lower body block for the legs are used to facilitate sash cramping the legs in position, once a good fit at each joint has been ensured. A single 2in (50mm) nail will hold the legs in place while the cramps are being positioned and the pegs can later be glued into ½in (13mm) holes drilled through into the lower body block, two pegs to each leg (Plate 52).

The leg muscle blocks are glued in position at the top of each leg and, when dry, the tops are planed off flush with the top of the lower body block.

The four middle body blocks are glued in place on the lower body block, overhanging the latter by about ¼in (6mm) at each side to allow for the swell of the horse's belly. When this middle section is set the upper body block is fitted down centrally onto it and glued in place. It is important to make the upper body block sit well on the middle section and to this end some careful planing is required. The front and rear ends of the body blocks finish virtually in a line vertically, while at the sides the middle blocks project by about ¼in (6mm) at each side (Plate 53). Further wooden dowel pegs can be driven through to ensure secure fixing of top to middle, and middle to lower body blocks.

Fig 13 Scale drawing of large horse lower body block showing how it is notched at the corners for the splay of the legs

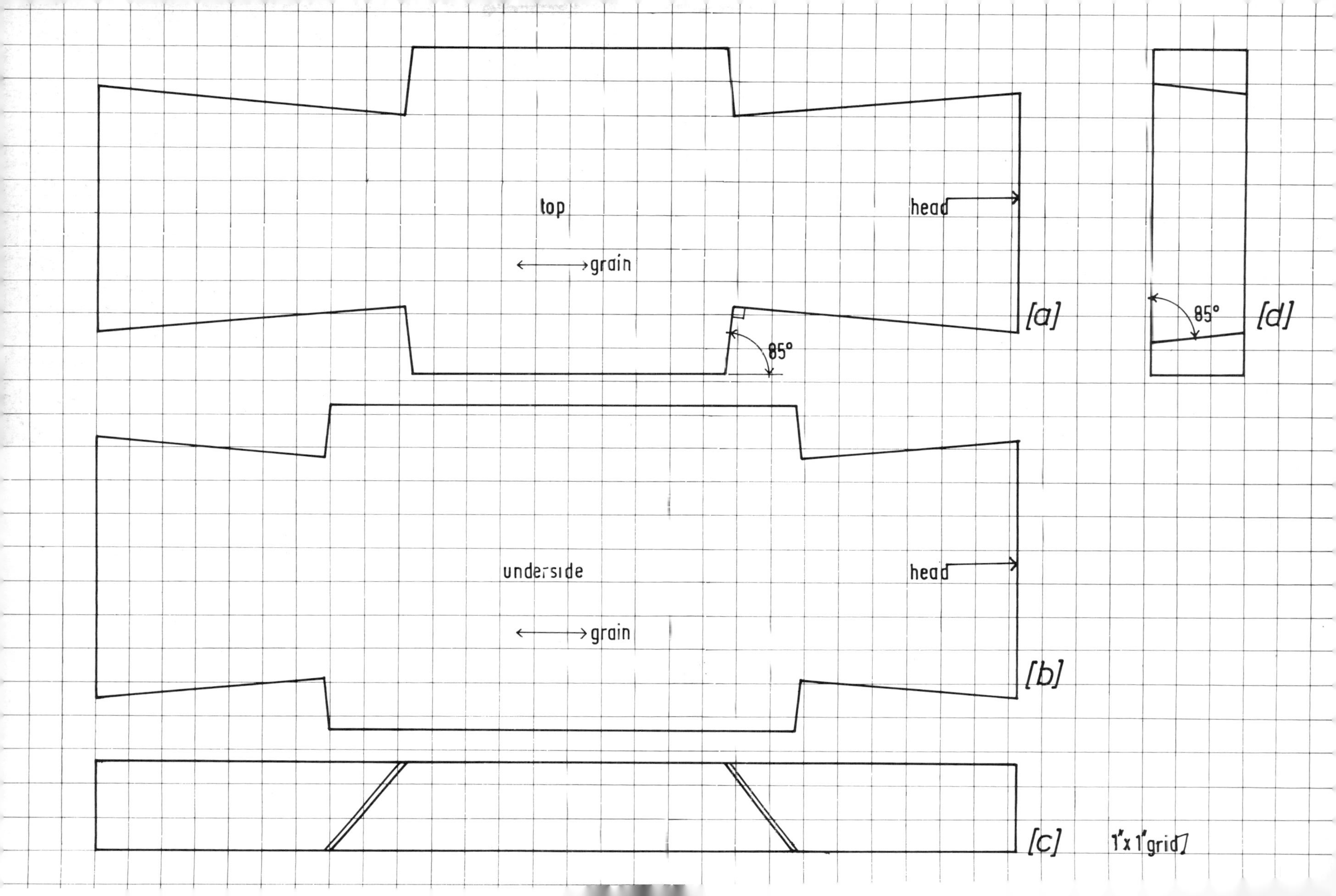
top
grain
head
85°
[a]
85°
[d]
underside
grain
head
[b]
[c]
[1"x 1" grid]

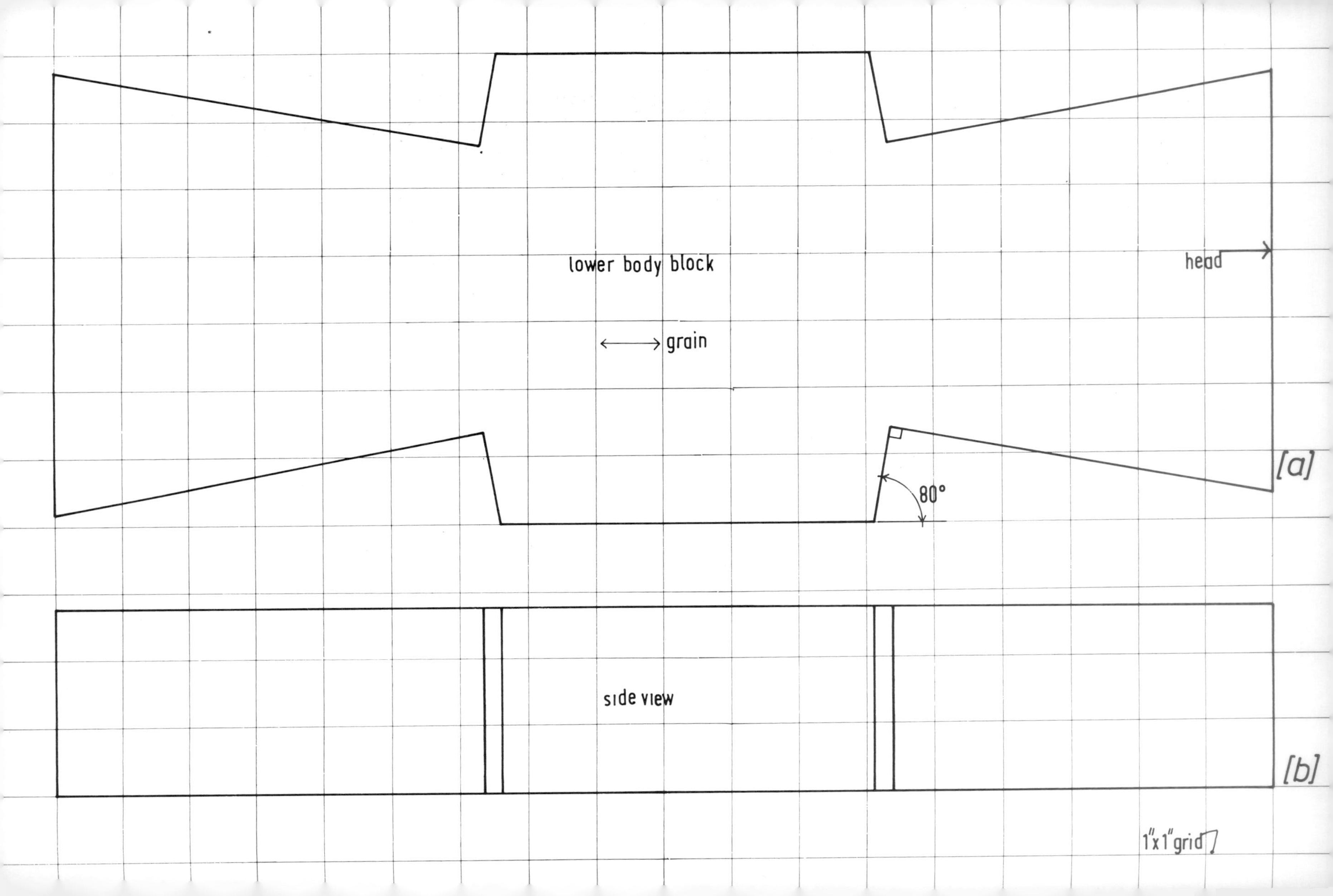
lower body block
grain
head
[a]
80°
side view
[b]
1"x1" grid

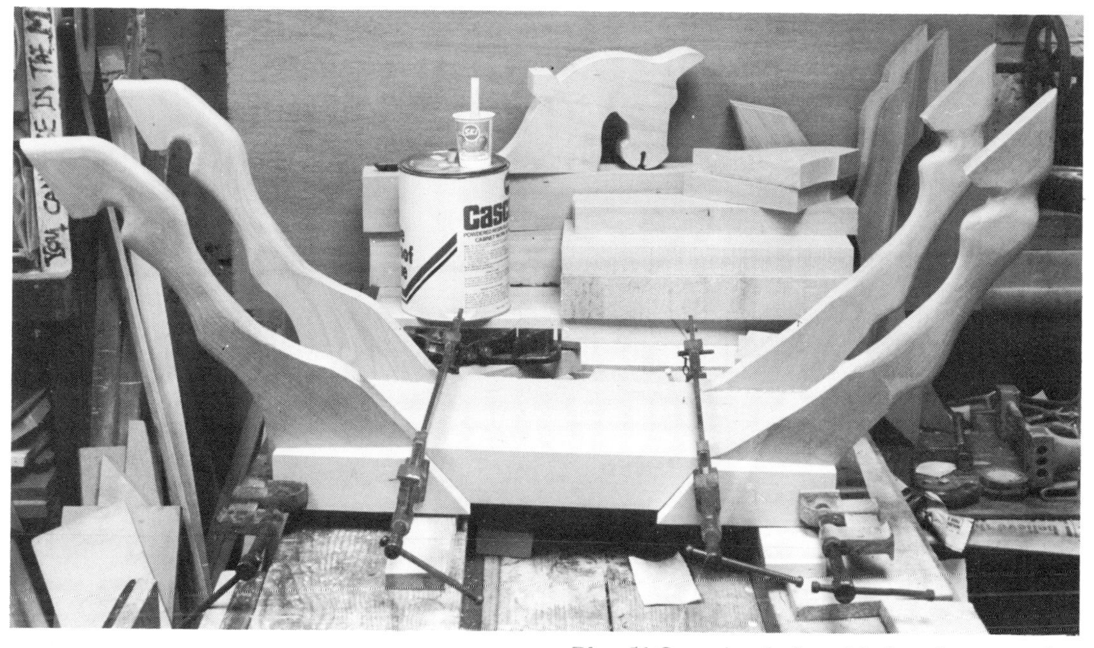

Plate 51 Cramping the legs of the large horse onto the lower body block

Fig 14 Scale drawing of the small fully-carved rocking-horse lower body block, showing how the corners are notched for the splay of the legs

Plate 52 The legs of the large and small horses shown glued and pegged onto their lower body blocks. The lower ends of the legs have been shaped prior to fixing

Plate 53 The final cramping together of the body blocks. All the blocks are glued in position and, when dry, the carving of the body can begin

Fig 15 Arrangement of blocks for the large rocking-horse

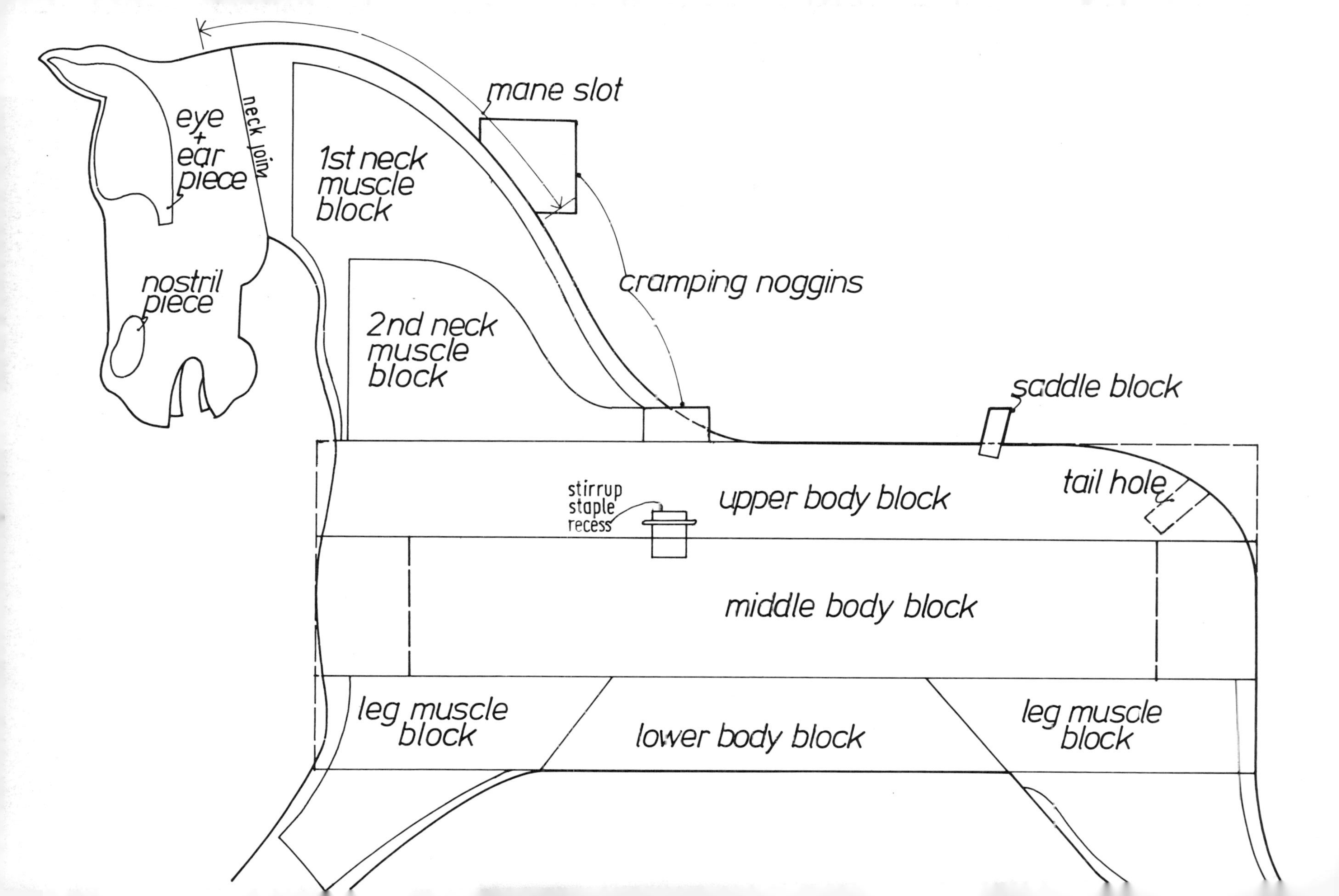
eye + ear piece
neck join
nostril piece
1st neck muscle block
2nd neck muscle block
mane slot
cramping noggins
saddle block
stirrup staple recess
upper body block
tail hole
middle body block
leg muscle block
lower body block
leg muscle block

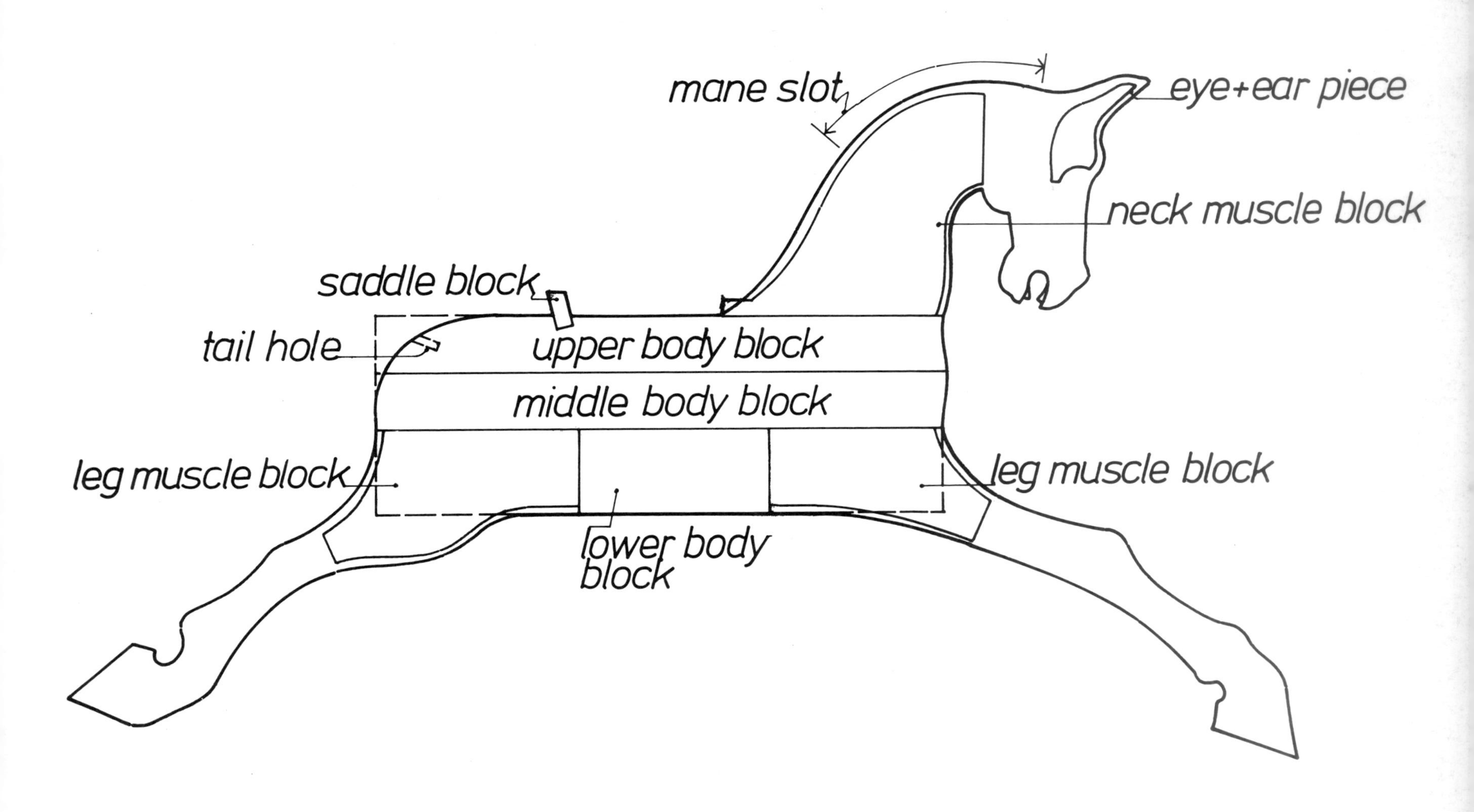
mane slot
eye+ear piece
neck muscle block
saddle block
tail hole
upper body block
middle body block
leg muscle block
leg muscle block
lower body block

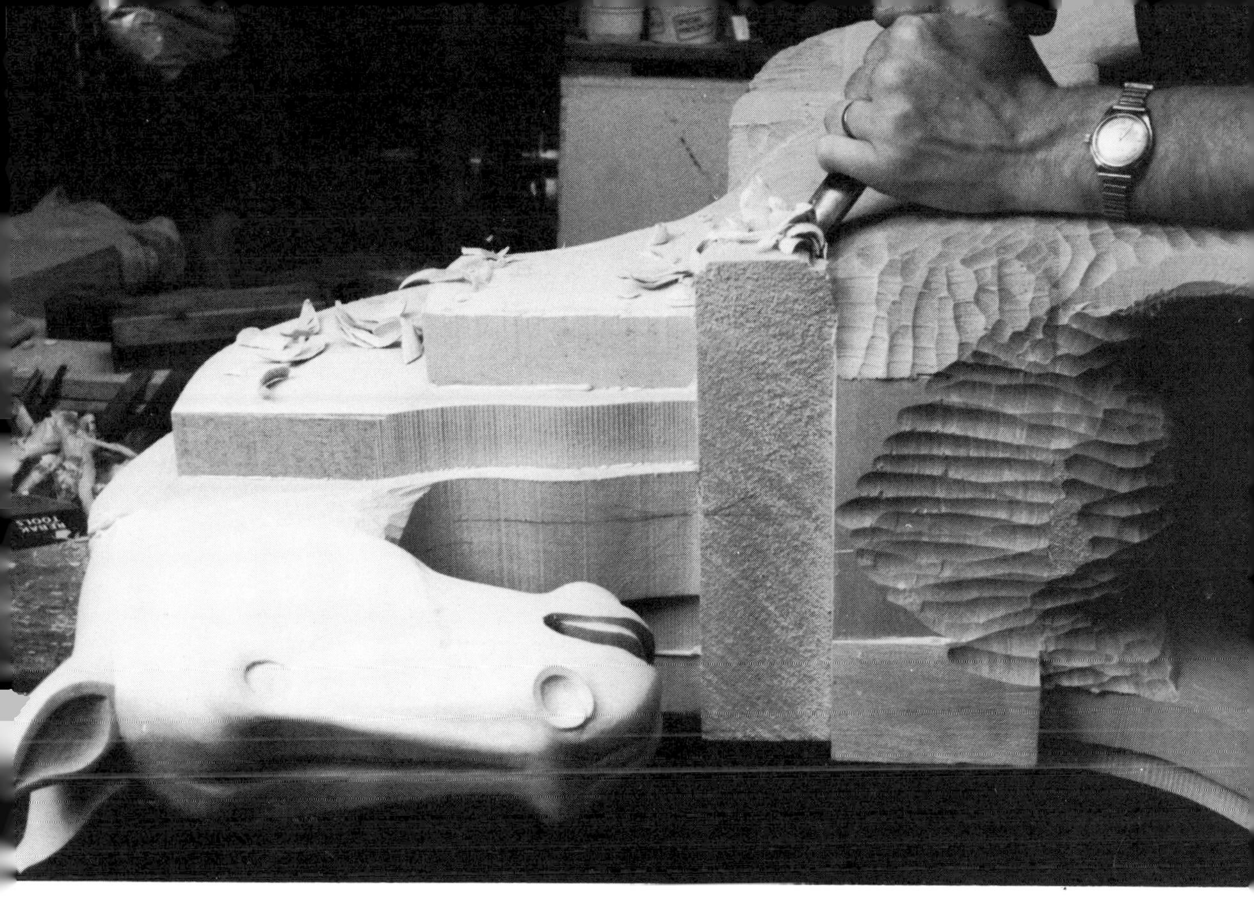

Plate 54 Rough carving the large horse. A 1in (25mm) straight gouge is being used to hack away the corners

That completes the assembly. You now have a hollow rectangular box with a horse's head sticking out of the top and four legs sticking out of the bottom corners (Figs 15 and 16). Start roughing out the shape of the body, neck and upper legs with a drawknife, continue with a large gouge and mallet, move on to smaller gouges, then finish with a spokeshave and finally glasspaper or sandpaper. Surforms are useful, particularly under the chin and round the tops of the legs. Larger pieces of waste wood, such as the area of the curve of the rump, can be removed with a hand saw. Do not be afraid of hacking in boldly and removing all trace of the ugly square box shape. It is impossible to describe in words the shaping of every contour of the horse, but the accompanying photographs should clarify the details. Note how the chest is hollowed out somewhat in the middle and the shaping around the tops of the legs (Plate 54). The neck should taper smoothly upward, becoming in cross section a series of progressively smaller 'egg' shapes until the muscle blocks merge with the central neck block in a clean curve behind the carving of the cheeks. Some suggestion of the muscling of the neck may be carved in.

Fig 16 Arrangement of blocks for the small fully-carved horse

Additional Details

After the main carving is completed, there remain a few details to add.

Saddle block The rear of the leather saddle will be fitted over a saddle block and this can now be fitted. It serves the purpose of raising the rear of the saddle (or cantle), making a more secure seat for a child, and is fitted into a groove cut across the horse's back and angled backwards slightly (Plate 59). Two saw cuts are made across the horse and the groove is chiselled out with a ½in (13mm) bevel-edged chisel. The saddle block is then glued and nailed securely in place, the ends shaped to run smoothly into the horse's body at each side.

Mane groove The mane will be fixed into a groove cut along the horse's neck. This groove is about ½in (13mm) deep, ¼in (6mm) wide and starts in the centre of the horse's neck an

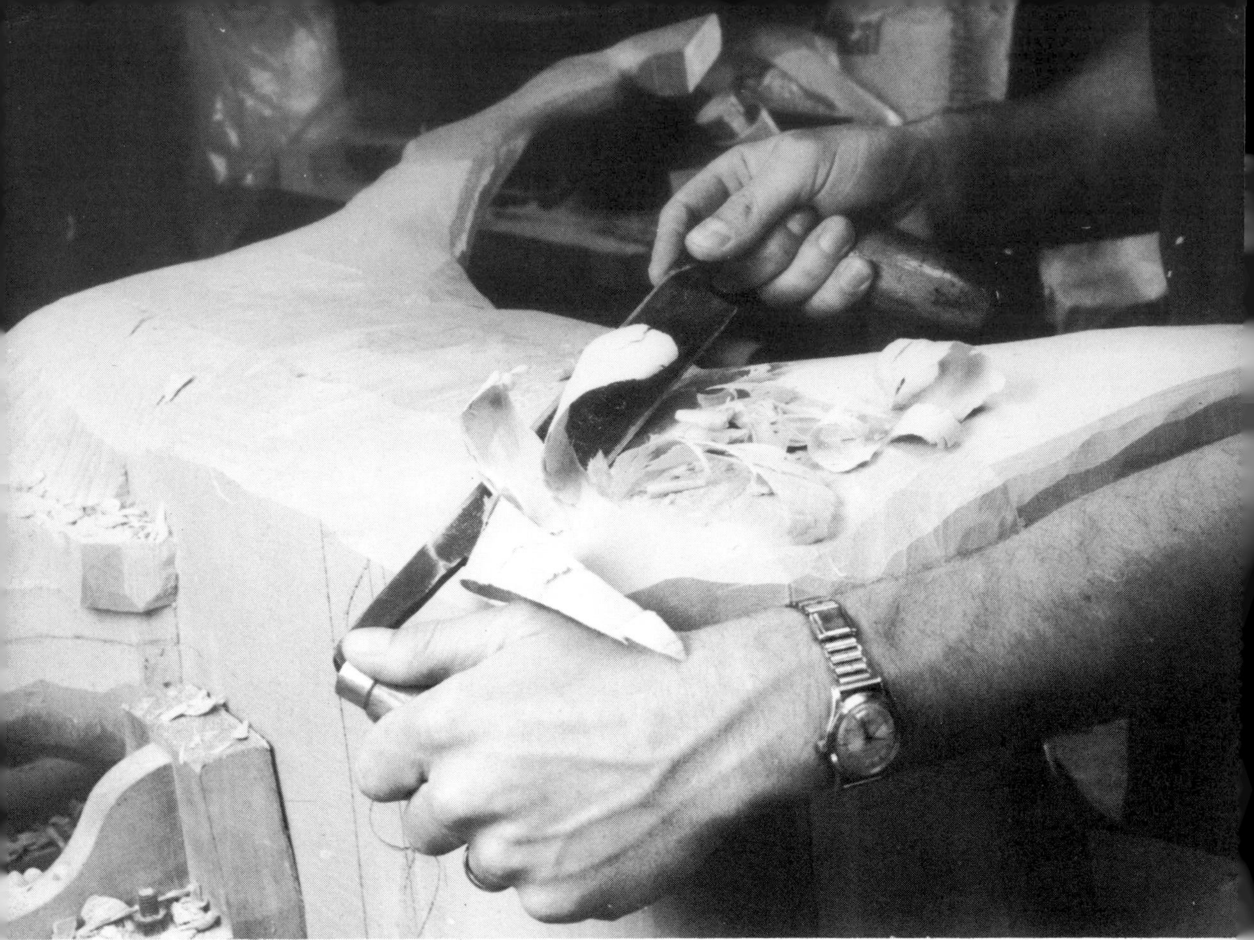

Plate 55 (above) Using a drawknife to cut away waste round the rump

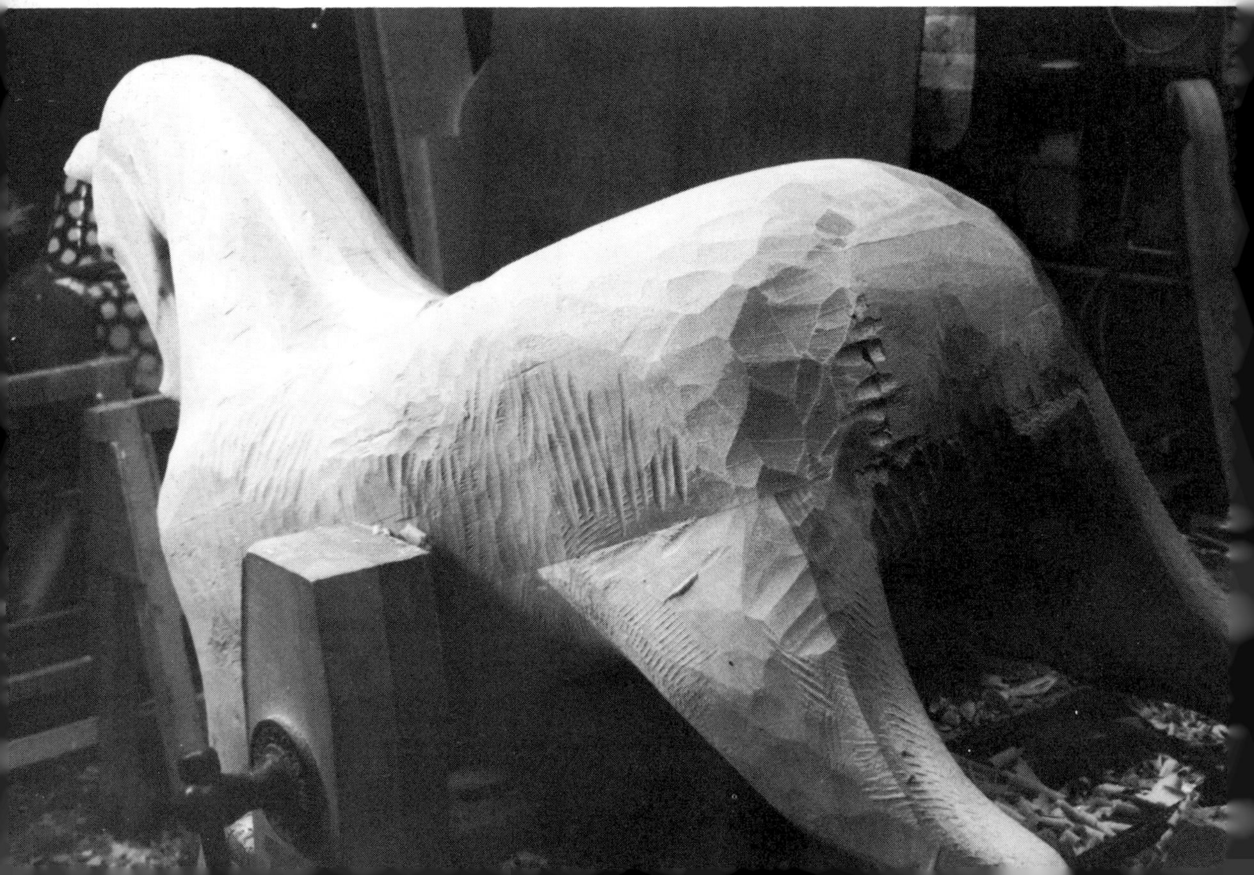

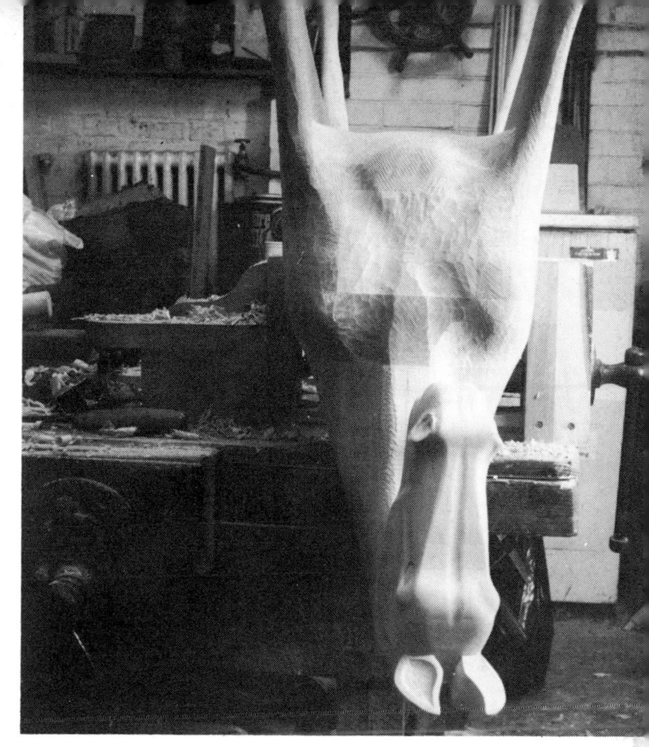

Plates 56 (opposite bottom) and 57 (above) The rough carving stage nearly complete. From this point on a curved surform and the spokeshaves will be used to get rid of the gouge marks and complete the detail of the curves

Plate 58 The large horse held firmly upside down in the carver's chops

Plate 59 Fixing the saddle block in a groove cut across the horse's back

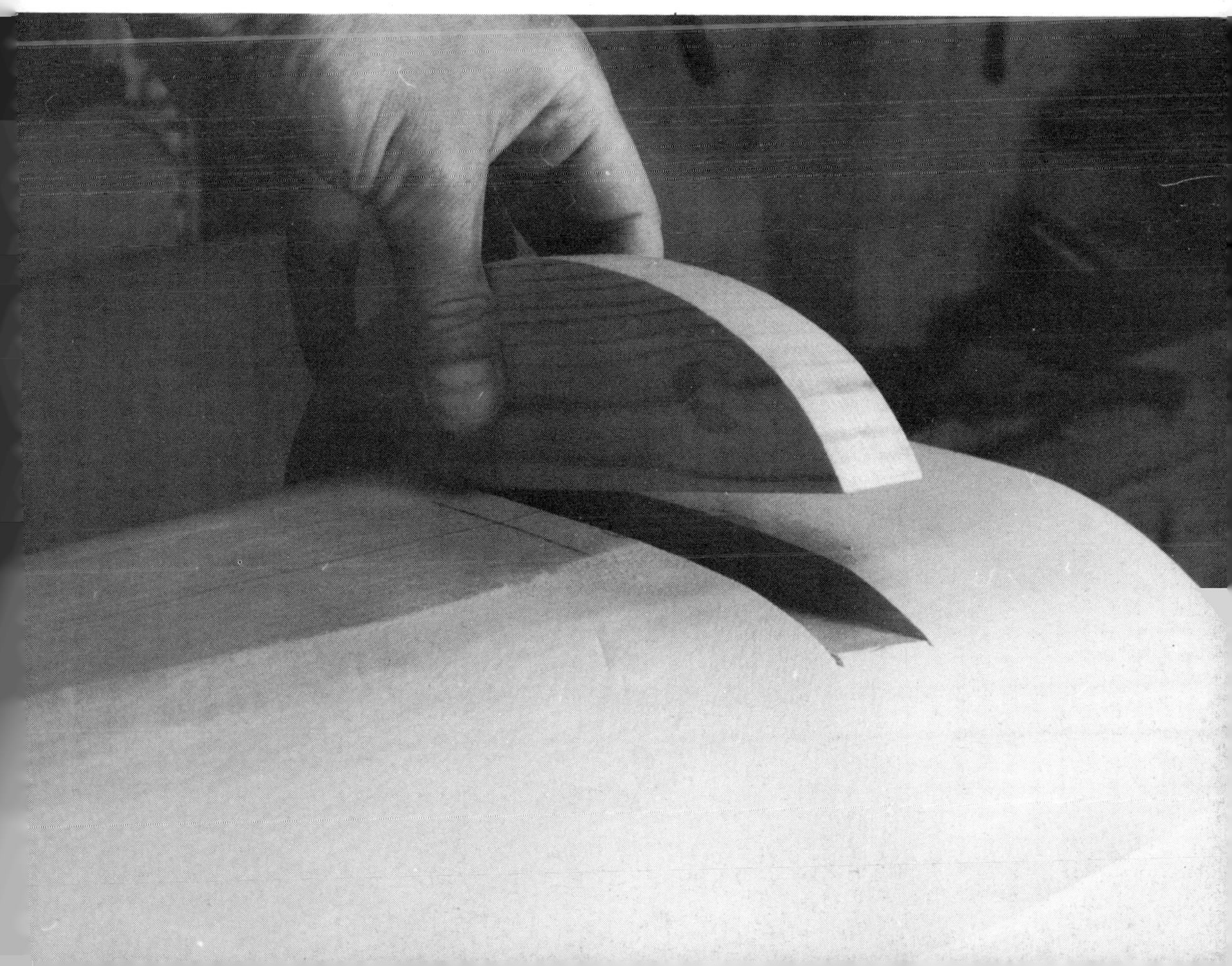

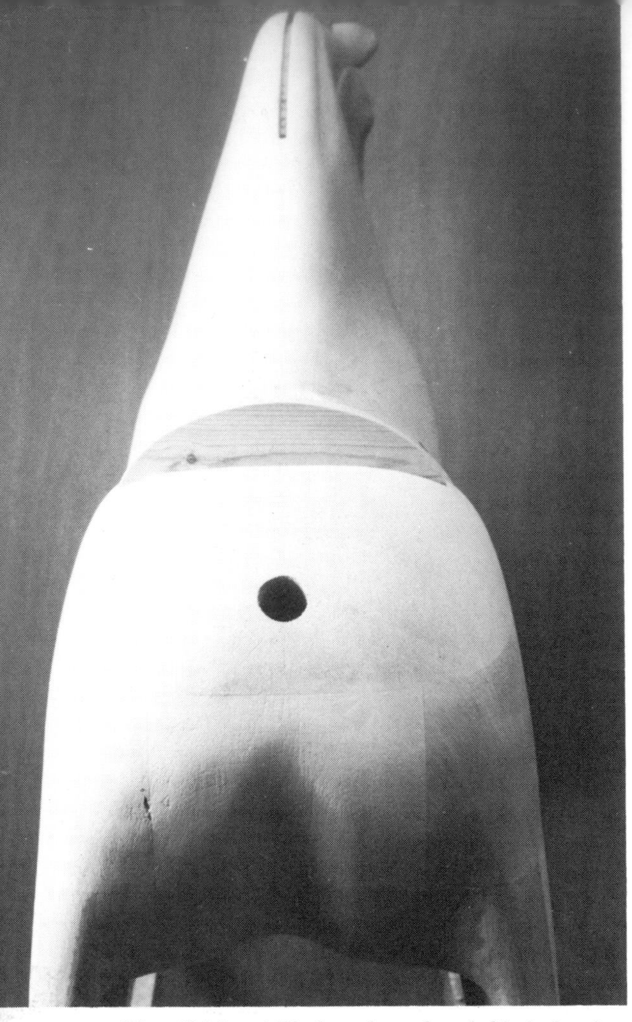

inch (25mm) or so behind the base of the ears. It runs back along the centre of the neck for 10½in (265mm) for the large horse, and 7in (180mm) for the small horse. The line of the groove is first pencilled in and then a series of ¼in (6mm) holes drilled to a depth of ½in (13mm). A piece of sticky tape wrapped round the bit will serve as a depth guide. The groove is chiselled out with a ¼in (6mm) chisel.

Tail hole The tail hole, ¾in (19mm) diameter, is drilled 1½in (40mm) deep at right angles to the horse's rump (Plate 60).

Stirrup staples On the larger horse the stirrups are hung from giant staples (see page 77) set into recesses cut into each side of the horse (Plate 61). This is done so that the buckles of the stirrup straps will be positioned in each of these recesses, the saddle flaps covering them, thus protecting the child's legs from rubbing against the buckles. The recesses are cut about ⅝in (16mm) deep with a 1in (25mm) drill bit and chisel and the giant staples driven in. Ensure that you leave sufficient gap beneath the staple to allow the stirrup leather to be threaded through.

Stirrup staples are not used on the smaller horse where a different saddle and stirrup strap arrangement is employed (see page 79).

Eyes The eyes should be glass — plastic is a

Plate 60 (above) The large horse from behind, showing tail hole, saddle block and mane groove

Plate 61 (below) The large horse: detail of stirrup staple and its recess

poor substitute. If they have wires these should be nipped off and the backs roughened slightly with a file before they are glued in place in their recesses with contact adhesive (see Appendix 3 for suppliers).

Notching the Hooves

The insides of the horse's hooves are notched to enable the horse to be fitted securely onto the cross struts, upon which the larger horse is mounted, or, in the case of the smaller horse, to fix it directly onto the sides of the rockers.

Large horse (Fig 17) The horse should be placed on a flat surface, and packing pieces 1/4in (6mm) thick placed under each hoof. Two lengths of 1in x 2in (25mm x 50mm) wood (temporary cross struts) are placed on edge along the inside of each pair of hooves, left and right. Take a pair of compasses opened to about 5/8in (16mm) and, holding the compasses horizontally with the compass point rubbing on the temporary cross strut, scribe on each hoof in turn the shape of the cross strut. These notches can then be cut out with a hand saw. Do ensure that the hoof ends are not cut too thin or they will be weakened. The horse will be held in place on the finished cross struts by a single 1/4in (6mm) carriage bolt at each hoof. Drill for these and bolt on the temporary cross struts or small pieces of scrap wood at this stage. This enables the horse to be moved around the workshop without danger of the tips of the hooves being chipped on the floor. After the horse has been painted this temporary mounting will be replaced by the proper varnished beech cross struts.

Small horse Notching the hooves of the smaller horse is more awkward and can only be done after the rockers have been assembled (see pages 93-7). The rockers are chocked up on the bench top and the horse is placed on a box or other support over the rockers so that each hoof just touches the rocker sides. The distance between the front hooves and the front end of the rockers should be about 2in (50mm) greater than the distance between the rear hooves and the rear end of the rockers. This ensures that the extra weight of the horse at the front (head and neck) does not make the horse tilt forward when standing at rest. The notches are then scribed onto the hooves as described, and cut out with a hand saw. Pieces of scrap wood are bolted on at each hoof, to keep the hooves off the ground while the painting and finishing goes on.

Gesso and the Paintwork

People who have had a chance to closely examine an old rocking-horse are sometimes surprised to find that beneath the surface of the paint the woodwork is covered with 'plaster'. This is not plaster, but gesso — a mixture of animal glue and whiting (ie fine chalk) which has been applied over the horse to provide a very hard, tough, smooth surface over which the paintwork can be laid (Plate 62). Without practice, gessoing can be difficult — it is rather like making bread in that although the ingredients and method are simple, it is easy to get it wrong. Details about the mixing and application of gesso are given in Appendix 2. Many people prefer to paint straight onto the wood after filling up any blemishes with some proprietary wood filler and using a grain sealer.

The method of painting described here is for a traditional dapple grey. Though other colour schemes, brown, black, palomino etc, and even varnished and polished natural wood

Plate 62 After gessoing the horse can be painted

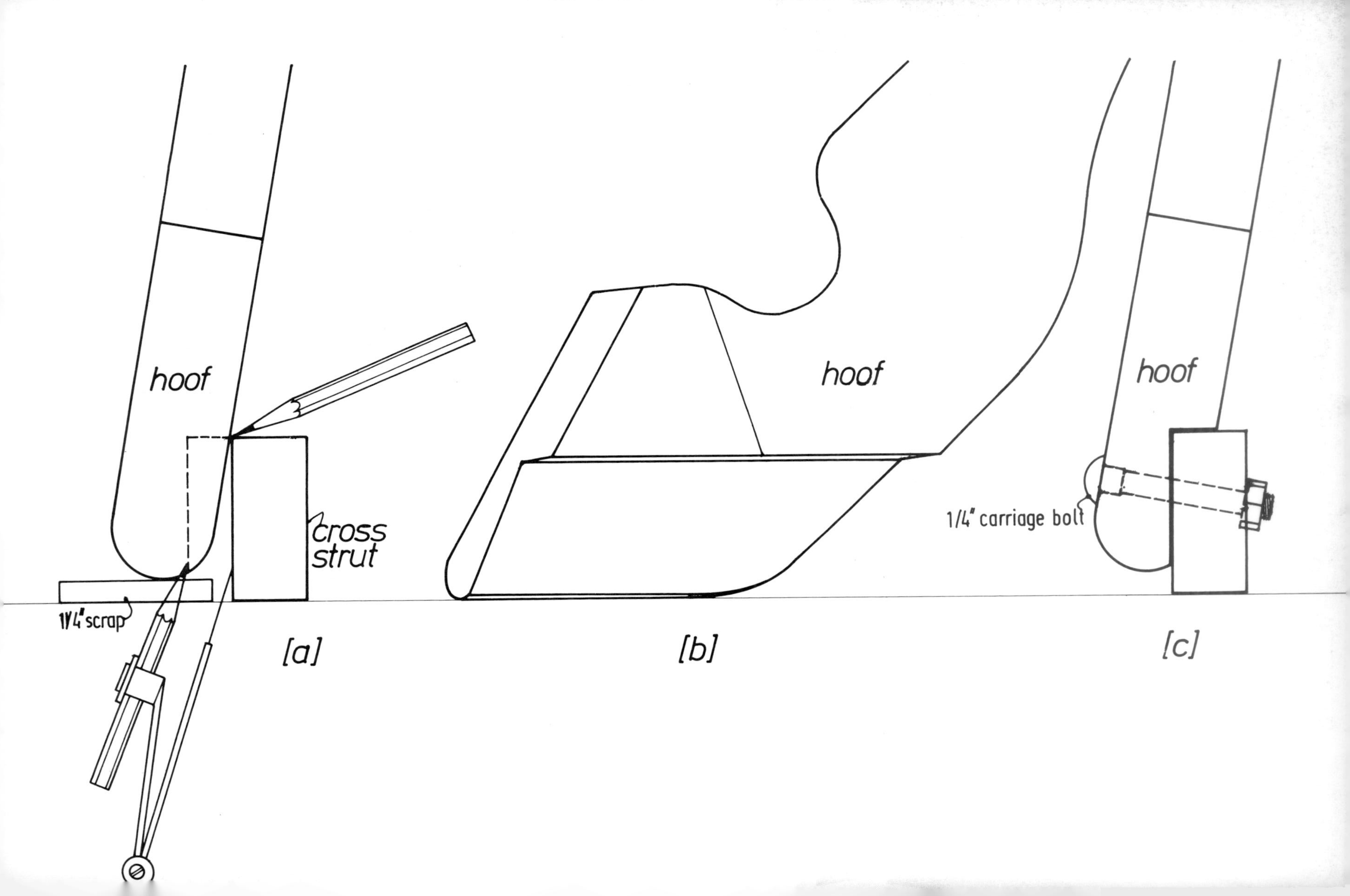
hoof
cross
strut
1 1/4" scrap
[a]
hoof
[b]
hoof
1/4" carriage bolt
[c]

Plate 63 The small horse, painted grey after gessoing. Then comes the final painting, starting with the ears, eyes, nostrils, mouth and hooves

finishes are possible, to my mind the proper finish for a traditional style rocking-horse is the dapple grey. A varnished wood finish is probably really appreciated only by adults; bright paintwork is more in tune with a child's appreciation of the rocking-horse. The basic colour is grey and a light grey lead-free shade should be chosen; a primer should be applied first, followed by three or four undercoats, topped off with two or three coats of gloss (Plate 63). Some people use only flat or matt paints, finishing with a coat of clear varnish, but varnish does tend to yellow with time.

When the horse has been painted entirely grey and has dried the dappling is laid on. Take a piece of fine muslin and make a small pad by wrapping it round a piece of foam rubber. Smear some black gloss paint onto a clean scrap of wood or an old tile. Press the dappling pad into the paint and then dab onto the horse (Plate 64). The pad will leave on the horse a distinctive 'hairy' pattern formed by the weave of the muslin. At first the pad will leave a lot of black but as the paint is used up it lightens, so start at a place where you want a lot of black and work towards the lighter areas.

Fig 17 (a) Scribing the hooves to notch them (b) so they sit over the cross strut (c). At (c) the nut is tightened so that it digs into the wood and no washer is needed

Work with a dabbing motion — do not smear the paint or you will make a mess of it, and dab in circles to leave clear grey spots. It is not vital that the dappling on one side of the horse is exactly matched by that on the other side, but the horse will look more satisfactory if the markings are roughly symmetrical, especially on the head. For alternative dappling methods, see page 114.

The hooves are painted in black and I paint in eyelashes and rim the eyes in black also. The insides of the ears and nostrils, and the mouth, are normally red, the teeth are white (Plates 67 and 68). Any paint that has gone over the glass eye can be carefully scraped off.

Harness and Saddlery
List of Requirements

Large Horse

One bit (mild steel with brass harness rings)
60in x ½in wide (1,525mm x 13mm) leather strapping for bridle
36in x ½in wide (915mm x 13mm) leather strapping for reins

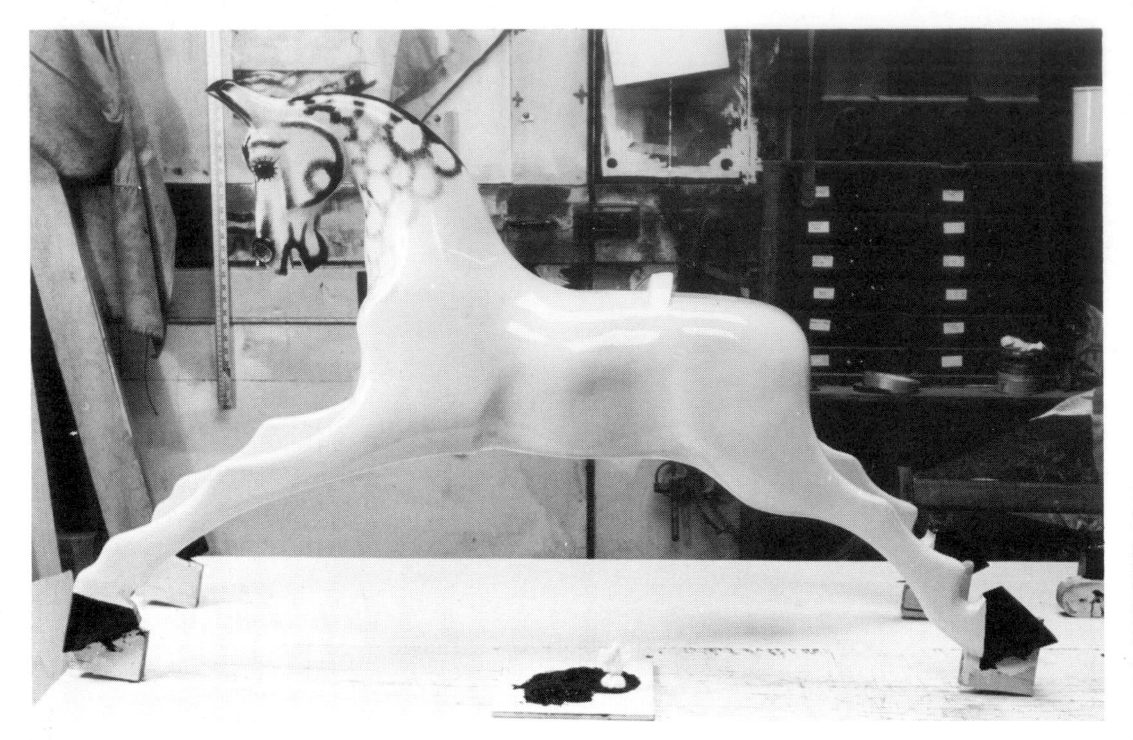

Plate 64 Dappling the small horse. The dappling pad is dipped into the black paint on an old ceramic tile

Plate 65 The small horse: dappling complete

Plate 66 The large horse: painting is now finished and dry, and the horse is ready for tacking up

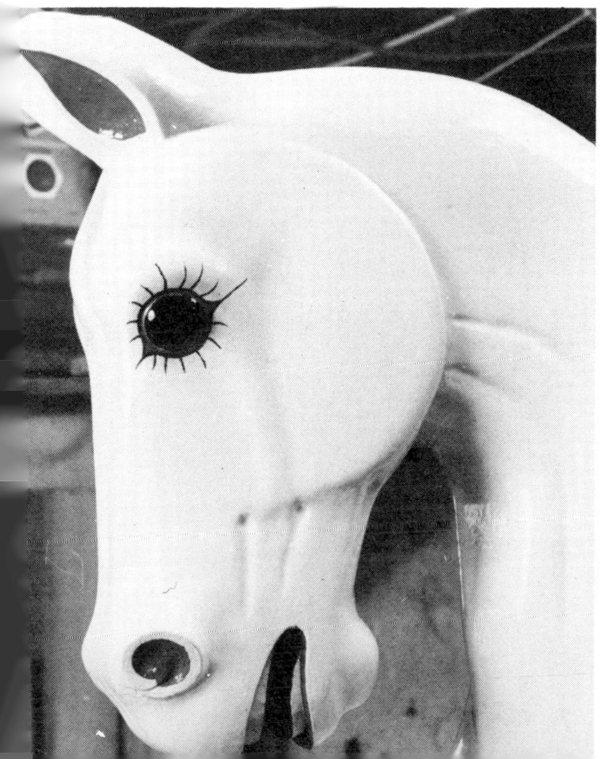

Plate 67 Painting in the nostrils, eyelashes, ears and mouth of the large horse

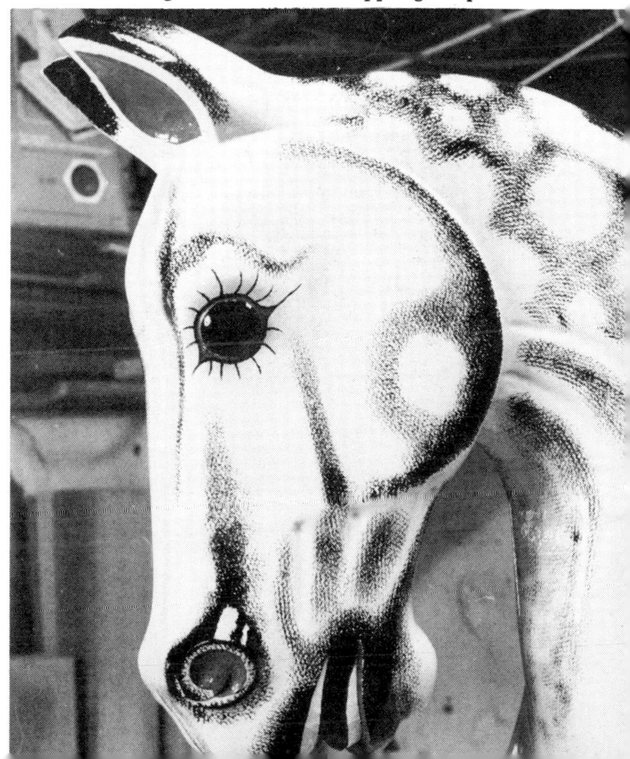

Plate 68 The large horse head with dappling complete

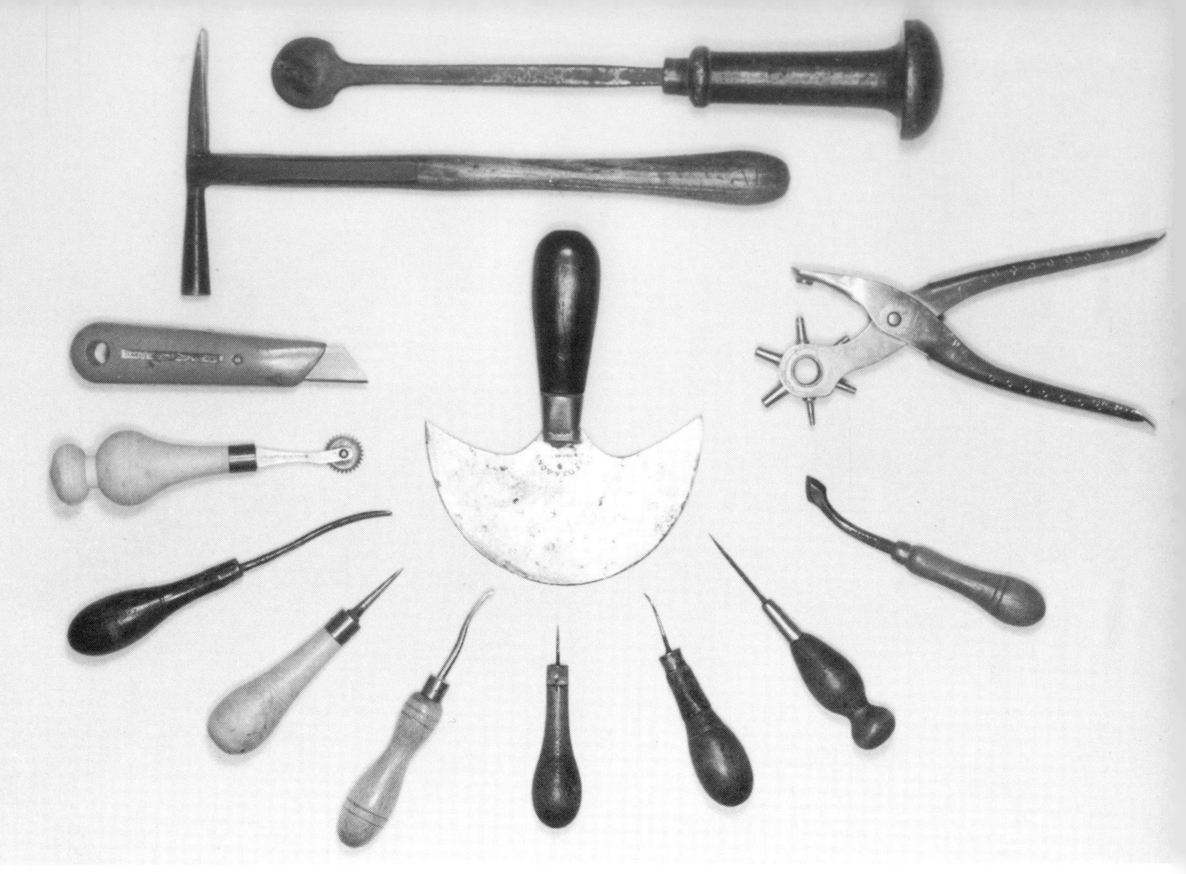

Plate 69 A selection of leather tools. In the centre, a head knife; bottom, shoulder vein; clockwise from the left, wheel-type hole punch, crease marker, three hole prickers, edge bevel, hole pricker, edge bevel, wheel-type stitch marker (not used on the bridles in this book), craft knife

Three 19in x ½in wide (483mm x 13mm) leather strapping for chest and tail straps
Three ½in (13mm) buckles for bridle
Two 24in x ¾in wide (610mm x 19mm) leather strapping for stirrup straps
Two ¾in (19mm) buckles for stirrup straps
Ten leather rivets
One pair stirrup irons — 3½in (90mm) sole are suitable
11in x 10in x 1/16in (280mm x 225mm x 1mm) leather for saddle top
19in x 17in (483mm x 432mm) leathercloth for saddlecloths
16in x 12in x ⅛in (406mm x 305mm x 3mm) leather for saddle flaps
One piece 2in (50mm) thick foam rubber for saddle padding
Seventy ½in (13mm) brass dome-headed nails
Fifteen ½in (13mm) fancy brass nails
One ⅝in (16mm) brass dome-headed nail
Two 1in (25mm) brass dome-headed nails

Small horse

One bit (mild steel with brass harness rings)
36in x ½in wide (915mm x 13mm) leather strapping for bridle
26in x ½in wide (660mm x 13mm) leather strapping for reins
Three 14in x ½in wide (356mm x 13mm) leather strapping for chest and tail straps
Two ½in (13mm) buckles for bridle
30in x ¾in wide (762mm x 19mm) leather strapping for stirrup straps
Two ¾in (19mm) buckles for stirrup straps
Eleven leather rivets
One pair stirrup irons — 2½in (64mm) sole are suitable
9in x 7in x 1/16in (230mm x 180mm x 1mm) leather for saddle
15in x 9in (381mm x 230mm) leathercloth for saddlecloths

Fig 18 Stirrup staples (a) made from 4in (10mm) nails. The head is sawn off and the end filed to a point. The staple is bent over in a metal vice. Bits for large horse (b) and small horse (c). The ⅛in (3mm) mild steel rod is first bent at right angles and the loops at each end forged after heating the ends with a blowtorch. Solid brass harness rings are slipped into the loop at each end before closing them up in a vice

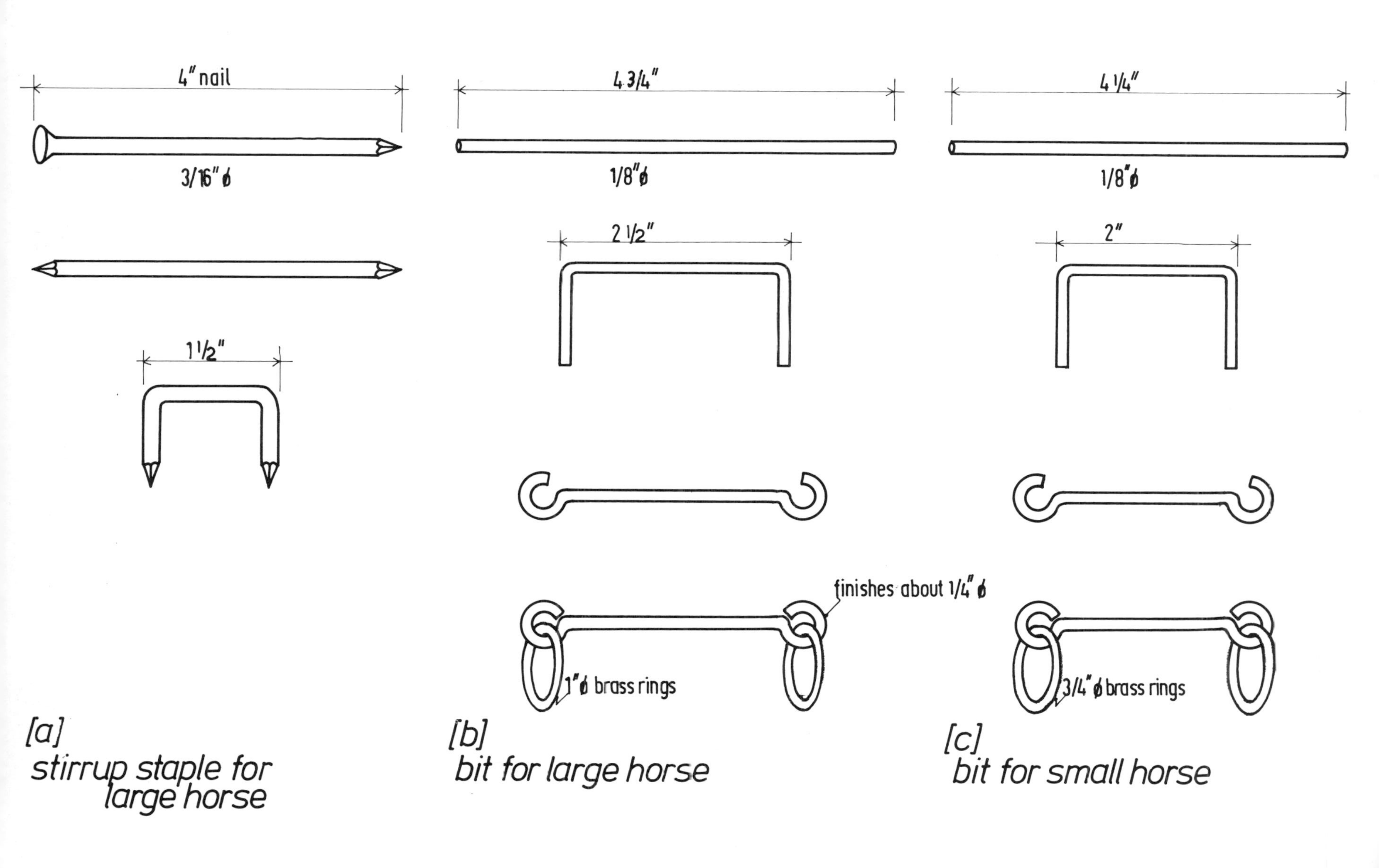

[a]
stirrup staple for large horse

[b]
bit for large horse

[c]
bit for small horse

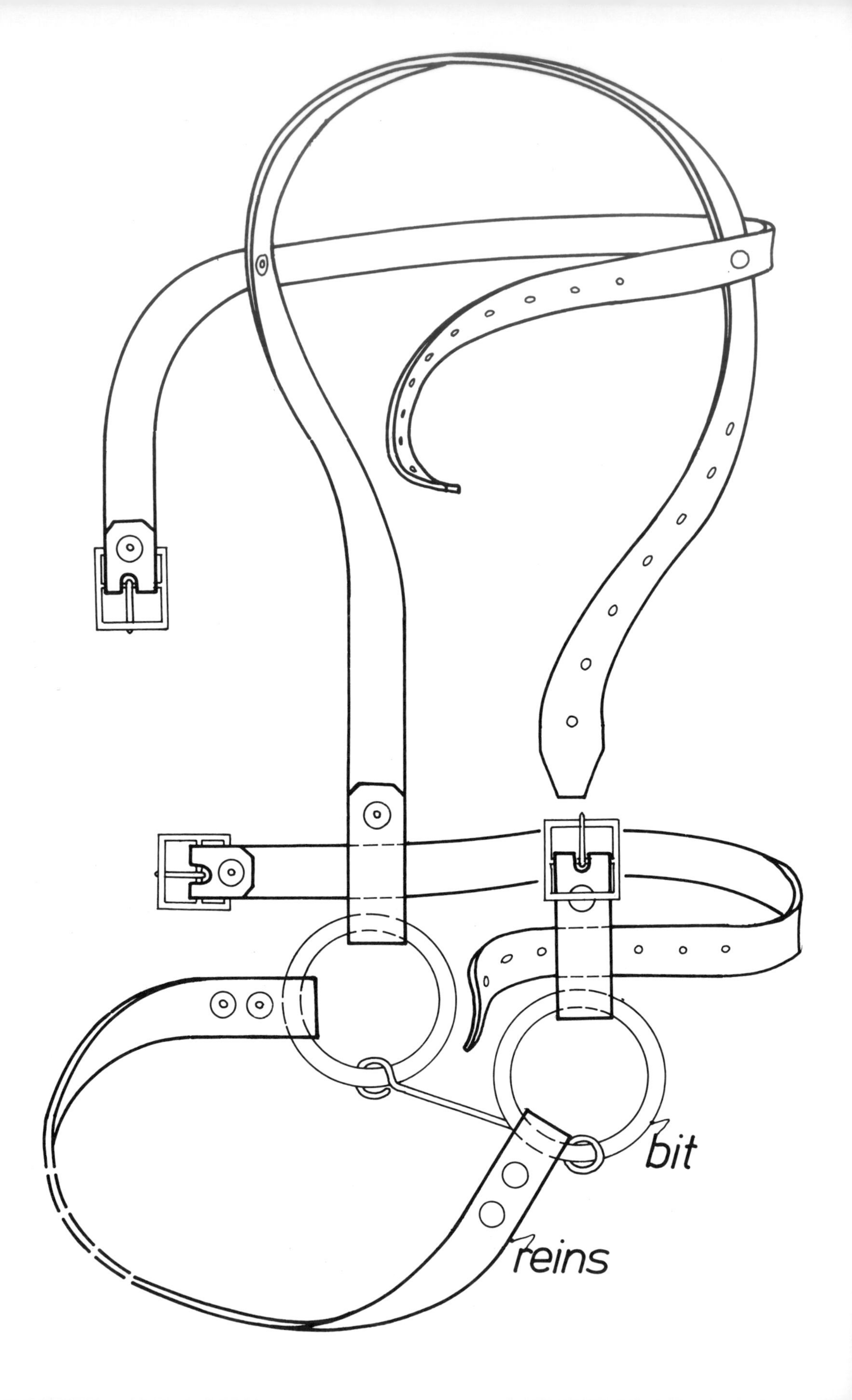
bit
reins

- One piece 1½in (30mm) thick foam rubber for saddle padding
- Fifty-five ½in (13mm) brass dome-headed nails
- Ten ½in (13mm) fancy brass nails
- One ⅝in (16mm) brass dome-headed nail
- Two ¾in (19mm) brass dome-headed nails

Having already invested a fair amount of time, energy and money in making the wooden horse, it would be a sad mistake to skimp on the finishing. Always use a really good quality saddle and harness leather which will be strong and lasting, and will eventually take on the pleasing patina of old leather polished by many small bottoms. Although some fine rocking-horses have removable saddles like miniature versions of real ones, most have the saddle nailed permanently in place and decorated with brass dome-headed nails. In this way there is no possibility of the saddle moving or slipping while the horse is being ridden.

On the other hand, if you use a bridle which is removable children can undo and replace it in their play. The horses illustrated in this book wear a simplified, miniature version of a real bridle held in place with small buckles. The bit is forged from ⅛in (3mm) steel rod with a solid brass harness ring at each end. Both bridle and reins are made up from ½in (12mm) wide leather strapping, about ⅛in (2mm–3mm) thick, as shown in the accompanying drawing (Fig 19), using brass leather rivets. Alternatively, bridles and saddles can be purchased ready made to fit your rocking-horse (see Appendix 3).

All the parts of the saddle are nailed onto the horse first with 1in (25mm) round wire nails the heads of which will later be hidden beneath the brass dome-headed nails. The saddlecloths are fixed first. These provide a bright splash of colour and are normally made of leathercloth, cut to shape and stretched tight across the horse's sides. They may be edged with some fancy braid if desired and should be fixed evenly at each side so that the top edge runs under the saddle (Fig 20). From here on the saddle and stirrup arrangements for the large and small horses are different.

Fig 19 Arrangement of the large horse removeable bridle made from ½in (13mm) wide leather harness strapping and small buckles, fixed together with leather rivets. The small horse bridle is similar except for the part of the upper strap which buckles under the horse's chin, which is omitted

Large horse saddle and stirrups A piece of the saddlecloth must be cut away to reveal the stirrup staples (Fig 18a) in their recesses beneath; the cut edge of the saddlecloth round these holes is nailed in place neatly. The stirrup straps are made up from ¾in (19mm) leather strapping, in this case like small belts, 24in (610mm) long with a buckle at one end and a row of holes at the other. The stirrup irons (see Appendix 3), either large rocking-horse stirrups or a small pony type, are threaded onto the straps which are in turn led round the stirrup staple from behind so that the buckle lies to the outside (Plate 70). After adjustment to suit the rider, the buckle should always be pulled back up to sit snugly in the recess cut for it, where it will be covered by the saddle flap, thus protecting the child's legs.

On this large horse the saddle flaps are cut from ⅛in (2mm–3mm) thick leather while the saddle is cut out separately from a piece of softer more supple ¹⁄₁₆in (1mm–1.5mm) thick panel leather. The saddle flaps are fixed at each side so that the pair touch together at the front. On the back of the saddle they are fixed at each end of and just in front of the saddle block. Make sure before nailing home that the saddle top will adequately cover the required area of the flaps so that no unsightly ends are left showing. The saddle top is fixed firmly over a piece of foam rubber about 2in (50mm) thick, cut so that it is about ½in (12mm) smaller all round than the saddle top and shaped to fit. Starting from the front of the saddle work round each side alternately with nails spaced at about 1¼in (32mm) intervals (Plate 71).

Small horse saddle and stirrups The ¾in (19mm) strap from which both stirrups hang is laid over the horse's back, just behind the point where the neck joins onto the body, and nailed in place in the middle so that it hangs down evenly at either side (Plate 72). Holes are punched at regular intervals from the ends of the strap. The stirrup irons, and the buckle which allows the stirrups to be adjusted up or down to suit the rider, are fixed to a short length of ¾in (19mm) leather as shown in the drawing (Fig 22).

The saddle and saddle flaps are cut all in one piece from soft panel leather about ¹⁄₁₆in

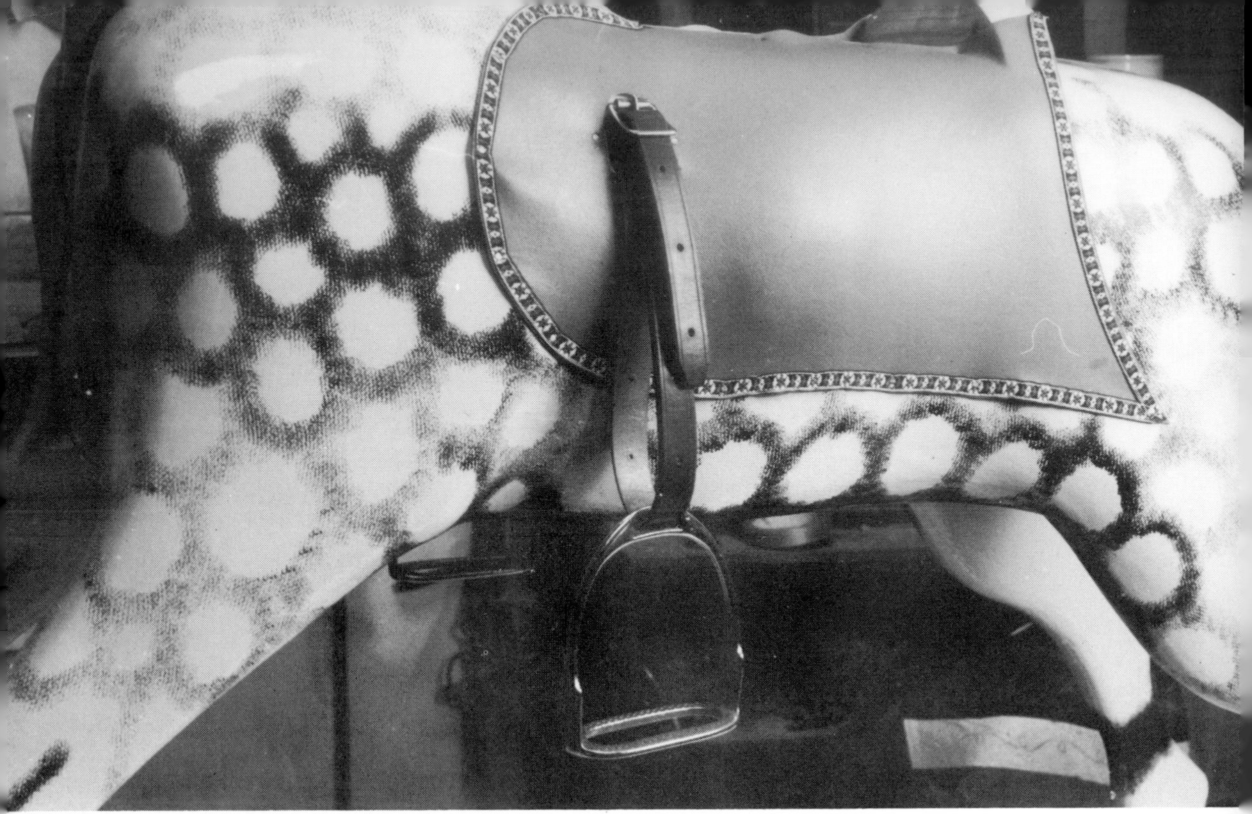

Plate 70 Tacking up the large horse: the saddlecloths are fixed first, then the stirrup straps are threaded through their staples

Plate 71 Detail of the large horse saddle complete

Fig 20 Saddle and harness arrangement (similar for large and small horses except as mentioned in caption to Fig 19)

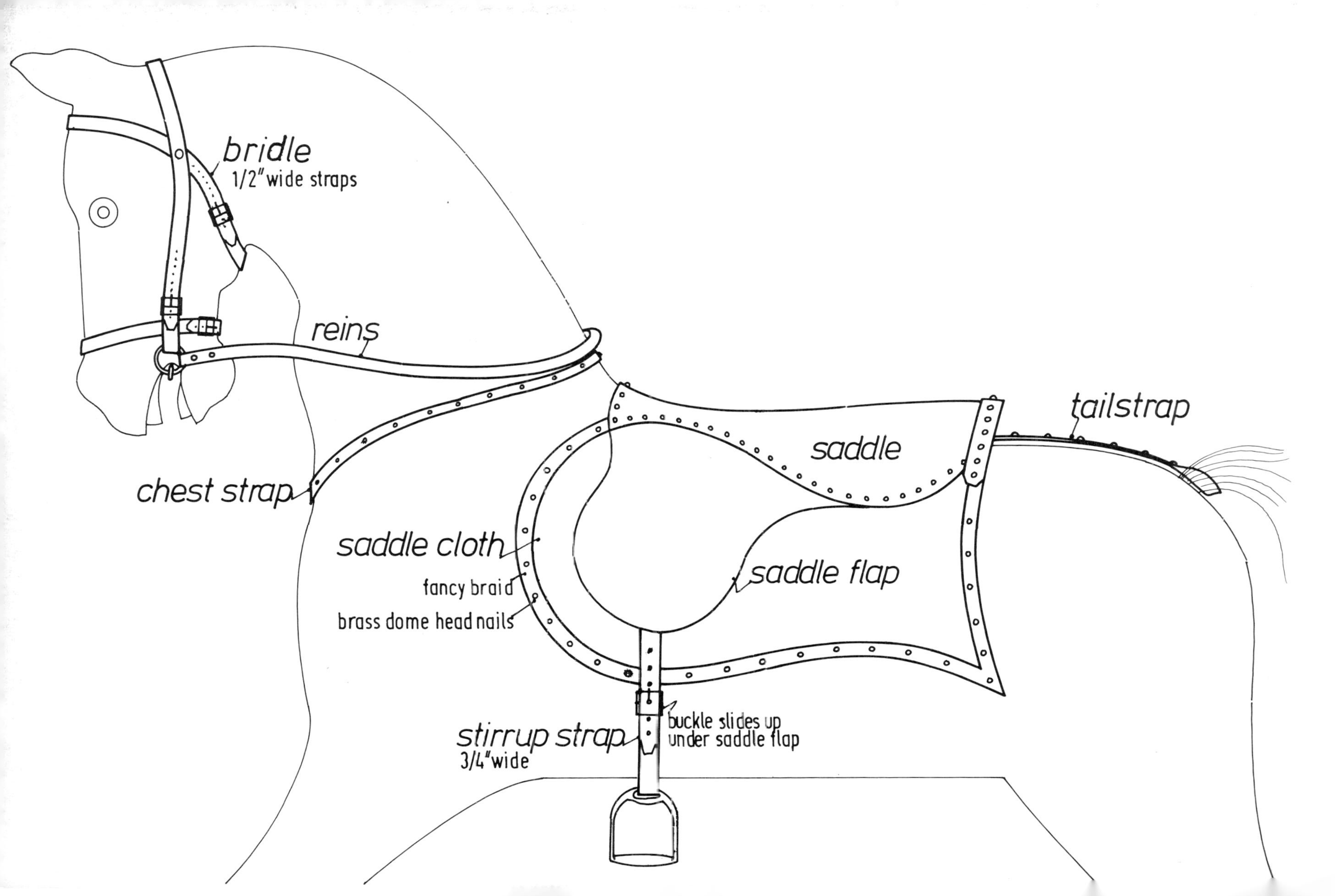
bridle
1/2" wide straps
reins
chest strap
saddle cloth
fancy braid
brass dome head nails
saddle
saddle flap
tailstrap
stirrup strap
3/4" wide
buckle slides up
under saddle flap

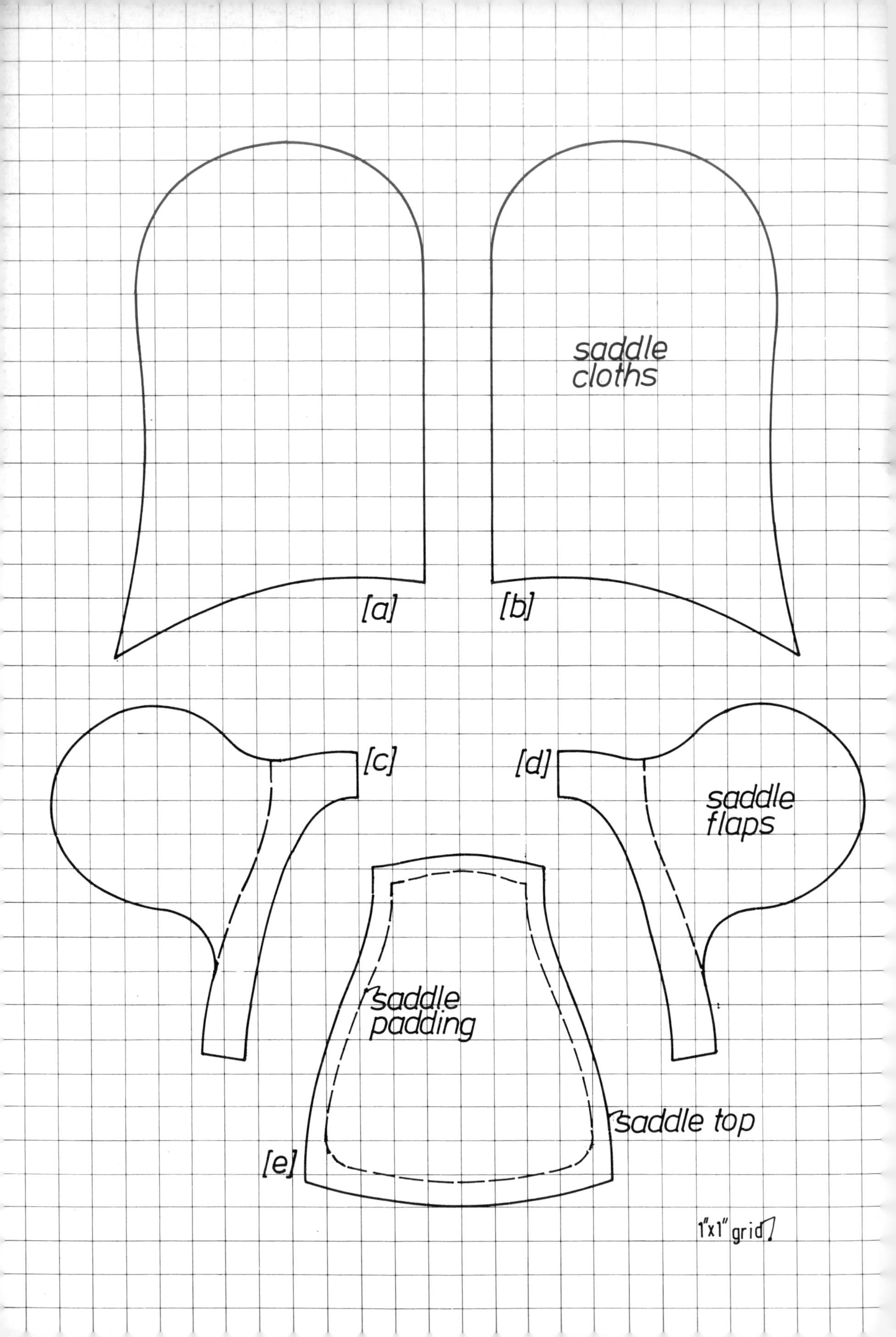

saddle cloths

[a]

[b]

[c]

[d]

saddle flaps

saddle padding

saddle top

[e]

1"x1" grid

Plate 72 Starting to tack up the small horse — saddlecloths first, then the stirrup straps

(1mm) thick. Cut a pad of foam rubber to fit under the seat and carefully nail the saddle in place, starting from the back centre of the saddle block and working round to the front end. The foam rubber padding should be 1½in or 2in (38mm–50mm) thick and is trimmed (ie bevelled) round the sides and front so it can be held firmly and neatly in place under the saddle top, providing a well padded seat for the child (Plate 73).

On both large and small horse saddles the heads of the 1in (25mm) round wire nails are hidden beneath brass dome-headed nails. These should be spaced as evenly as possible at 1¼in–1½in (32mm–38mm) intervals all round the edge of the saddle top, and along the edges of the saddlecloths (Plate 74).

A length of ½in (19mm) strapping is used as a chest strap. It is led round the neck, the ends converging in the middle of the chest.

Fig 21 Scale drawing of large horse saddle parts. The saddle cloths (a) and (b) are cut from brightly-coloured leathercloth; the saddle flaps (c) and (d) are cut from 1/8in (2.5–3mm) leather and the saddle top (e) cut from 1/16in (1mm) panel leather. The outline of the saddle padding, also shown in (e), is a piece of 1½in (38mm) thick foam rubber

From here a short length of the strapping is taken downwards and fixed under the horse. This chest strap (and the tail strap, see below) are decorated with brass dome-headed nails and fancy brass-headed nails alternately, spaced out at intervals of about 1½in (38mm). The point where the chest straps converge is hidden beneath a coloured rosette made from red and white ribbon.

Tail and Mane

Tails and manes are made from synthetic hair, using materials such as nylon, thick wool or some other substance roughly resembling horsehair. Choose a colour which is suitable for the colour of the horse's body; black and white for a dapple-grey rocking-horse, white for a palomino, brown for chestnut.

The tail is glued into the tail hole and, if necessary, a wooden wedge is driven in underneath to hold it securely in place. Take a length of ½in (19mm) leather strapping and fix the end immediately behind the saddle block in the centre. The other end loops round the base of the tail and is nailed in position, being finished off with brass-headed nails. This strap

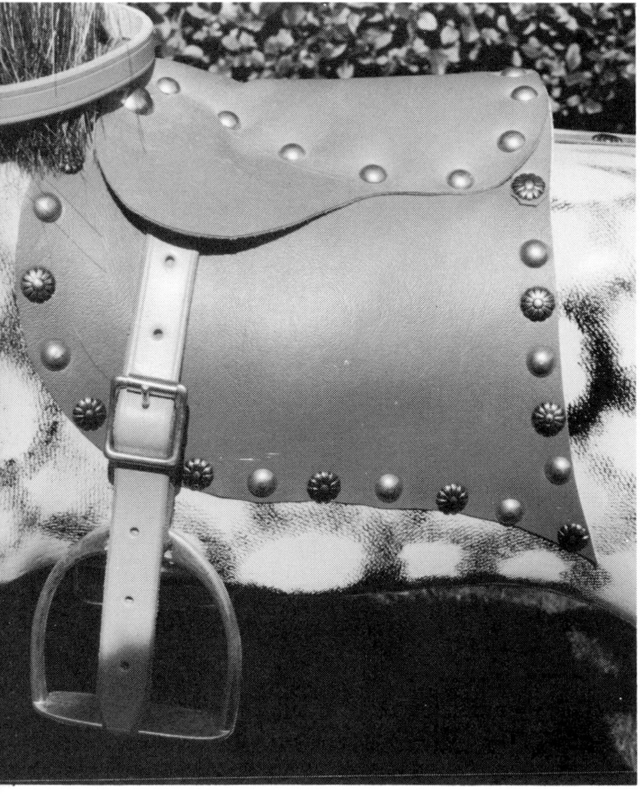

Plate 73 (above) The saddle is fixed over a foam pad and finished off with the brass nails

Plate 74 (left) Detail of the small horse saddle

hides any roughness round the base of the tail and helps to hold the tail up, which looks better.

It is very important to fix the mane in place in such a way that it is really secure, because children tend to hang on to the mane rather than the reins. I have found, after experimenting with various types of mane, that the best way is to use a long piece of mane material seamed down the middle and fixed into the mane slot as shown in the accompanying drawings (Fig 24). In this way the mane can resist considerable tugging. The 'hair' is led right round the first leather strip (24b), wedged in place in the slot with the second leather strip and nailed in fast (24c). A smear of glue along the seam will give extra security.

Fig 22 Stirrup strap arrangement as used on the small rocking-horse

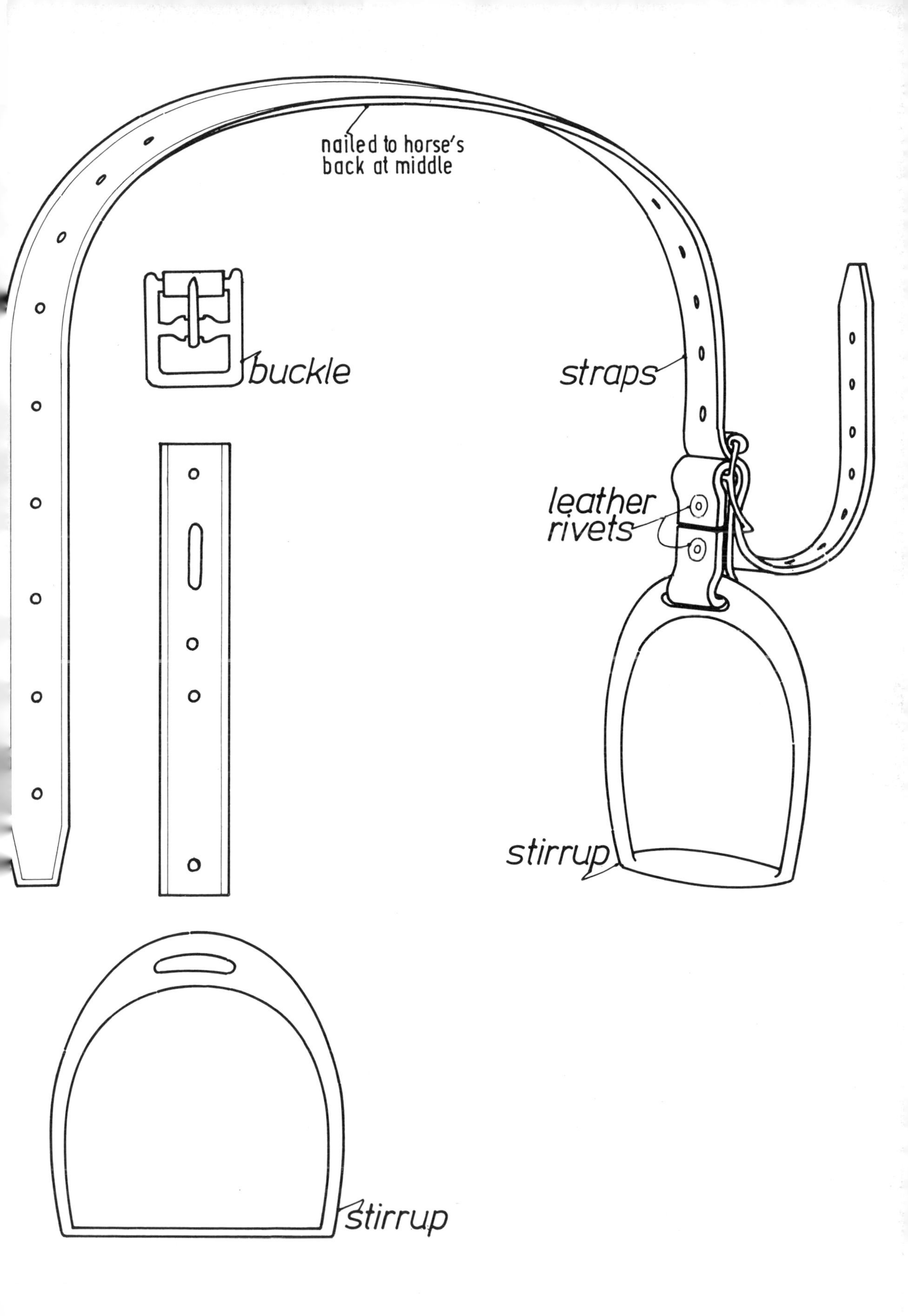
nailed to horse's back at middle
buckle
straps
leather rivets
stirrup
stirrup

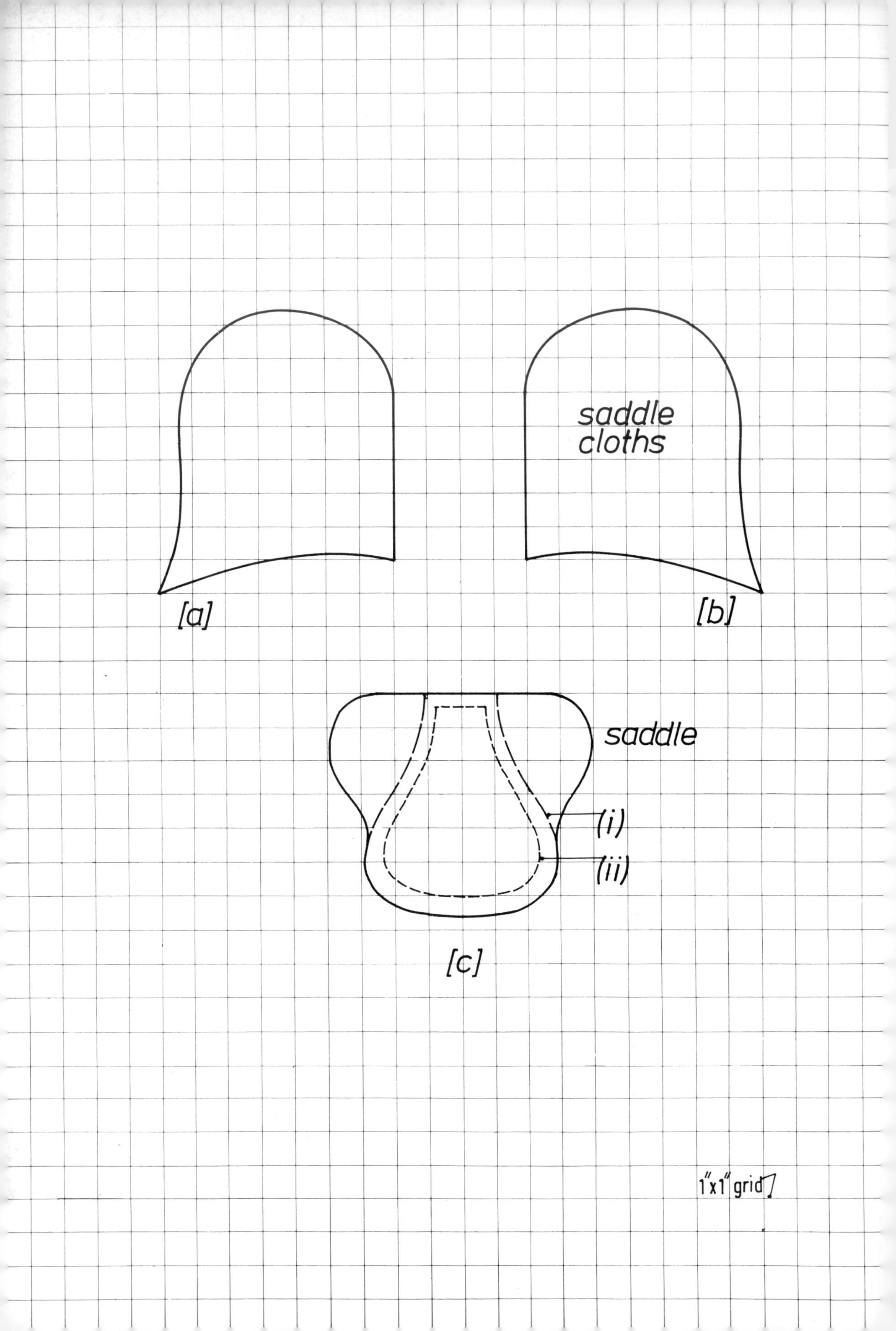
saddle
cloths
[a]
[b]
saddle
(i)
(ii)
[c]
1"x1" grid

Plate 75 (right) The small horse head complete with mane and bridle

Plate 76 (below right) The large horse head complete with mane, forelock and bridle

You will probably find that the mane sticks up at odd angles. This can be corrected by damping it slightly, laying a damp rag over the mane and tying it down in place, making sure that you take a bunch of 'hair' over the top of the head to hang down between the ears as a forelock (Plate 76). After having been left overnight the mane will remain in place and it can be combed out and trimmed as required.

Stands and Rockers

The Stand for the Large Horse

List of Requirements

- Wooden stand in Douglas fir (see scale drawings)
- Hand brace or electric drill and 1⅜in (35mm) twist bit or flat bit
- Pair of cross struts in beech, to which the horse's hooves will be bolted
- Twelve 1¾in (45mm) wood screws
- Pair of 7/16in (12mm) diameter swing irons in mild or bright steel with split pins and washers
- Pair of swing iron brackets, to fit swing irons
- Diameter ¼in x 1⅜in (6mm x 35mm) bolts and nuts for above brackets (six or eight will be needed according to the type of bracket used)
- Pair of steel bearing strips 4½in x ½in wide (114mm x 13mm)
- Four brass 'bowler hats'
- Details of where metal stand fittings may be obtained are given in Appendix 3

The construction of the wooden stand is quite straightforward. I use Douglas fir but pitch pine, parana pine, oak or other timber may be used quite satisfactorily. The stand consists of a top rail over which the swing irons hang, and

Fig 23 Scale drawing of small horse saddle parts. The saddlecloths (a) and (b) are cut from brightly-coloured leathercloth; the saddle top and saddle flaps (c) are cut from a single piece of 1/16in (1mm) thick panel leather. The broken line (i) indicates the line of the fixing nails and the broken line (ii) is the outline of the saddle padding which is a piece of 1½in (38mm) thick foam rubber

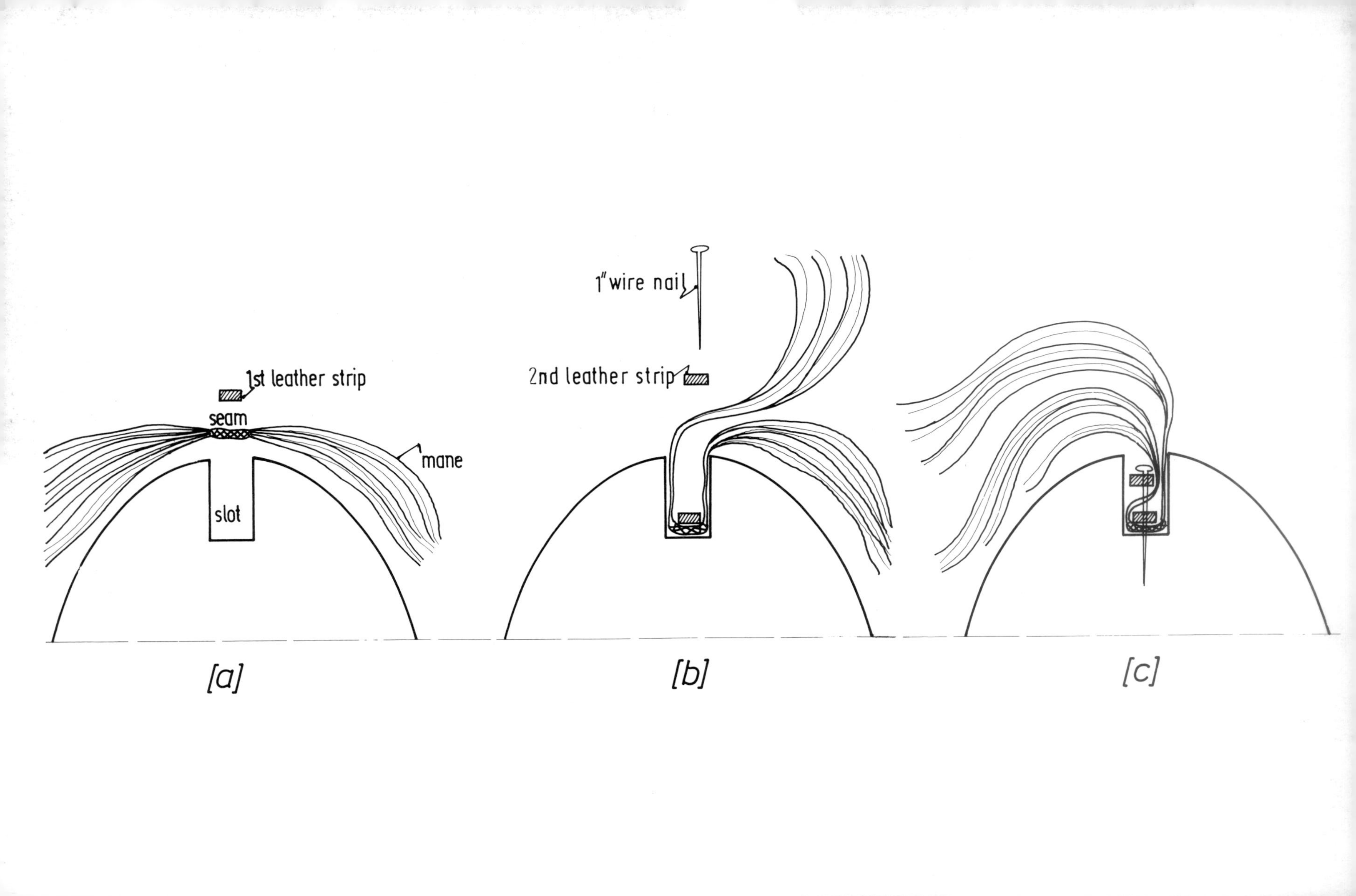
1st leather strip
seam
slot
mane
[a]
1" wire nail
2nd leather strip
[b]
[c]

a bottom rail, which has small pieces of wood fixed underneath at either end and is sufficiently long so as to prevent the horse from tipping over headlong when ridden hard. The cross pieces are glued and screwed up from underneath into the bottom rail and these prevent the horse from tipping over sideways. The upper edges of the stand — top, bottom and cross pieces — are all chamfered and sanded smooth and the ends of the top rail are rounded off. The ends of the stand posts pass through the top rail and right through the bottom rail and cross pieces, being glued and wedged firmly in place top and bottom.

The stand posts are best turned if you have access to a lathe — or perhaps a local craftsman will turn them for you (Plate 77). Many different patterns for stand posts have been used and a few examples of stand post designs are shown in Fig 27 (a–d). The ends are turned down to a diameter of 1⅜in (35mm) to form pegs which are fixed through holes of the same diameter drilled through the stand top and bottom. In the absence of a lathe the posts can be made of 4in (100mm) square section timber, tapered towards the top as shown in Fig 27(e) and cut to make tenons 1½in (38mm) square which fit into mortices cut in

Fig 24 Showing how the mane is fitted securely into its slot

Plate 77 A large horse stand post in the lathe

Plate 78 Fixing together the stand. Note the wedges in the top of each post

Plate 79 Cast brass swing iron bracket

the top and bottom of the stand — again glued and wedged in place (Plate 78).

The two cross struts to which the horse's hooves are bolted and through which the lower ends of the swing irons pass are made of beech rounded off at the ends, and a decorative chamfer cut into the mid section as shown in Fig 25. These and the stand are finished with three or four coats of varnish.

The swing irons cross the top of the stand 3in (75mm) from either end. To prevent them from wearing into the wood a strip of 22 or 24 gauge steel ½in (13mm) wide and 4½in (114mm) long is nailed over the stand top for each swing iron to bear upon (Fig 28). The swing iron brackets are positioned over the top and the holes, ¼in (6mm) dia., are drilled for later fixing (Plates 79 and 80). No washers need be used when tightening the nuts onto the bolts — the nuts dig into the wood and remain secure.

Due to small variations in the angling of the legs to the horse's body you will probably find that the front and rear hooves are not exactly the same distance apart. This is not important so long as, when fitted, the swing irons are not under stress. Consequently the lower ends of the swing irons should be adjusted by bending them in a vice, to match the distance apart of the cross struts, near the hooves front and rear. This measurement will be in the region of 13in (330mm), give or take an inch or so.

The lower ends of the swing irons pass through 7/16in (12mm) holes drilled in the cross struts and are secured with a washer and split pin (Fig 29). A dab of grease helps to prevent squeaking and an added refinement is to line the holes in the cross struts with a bush made from a piece of ½in (12mm) internal diameter steel or brass tubing to make a really long-lasting bearing. The split pins and washers look rather ugly so are hidden beneath small brass 'bowler hats' fixed in place with small round-headed brass screws. When the varnish has dried the horse can be removed from its

Fig 25 Scale drawing of large horse: (a) swing iron safety stand; (b) cross strut

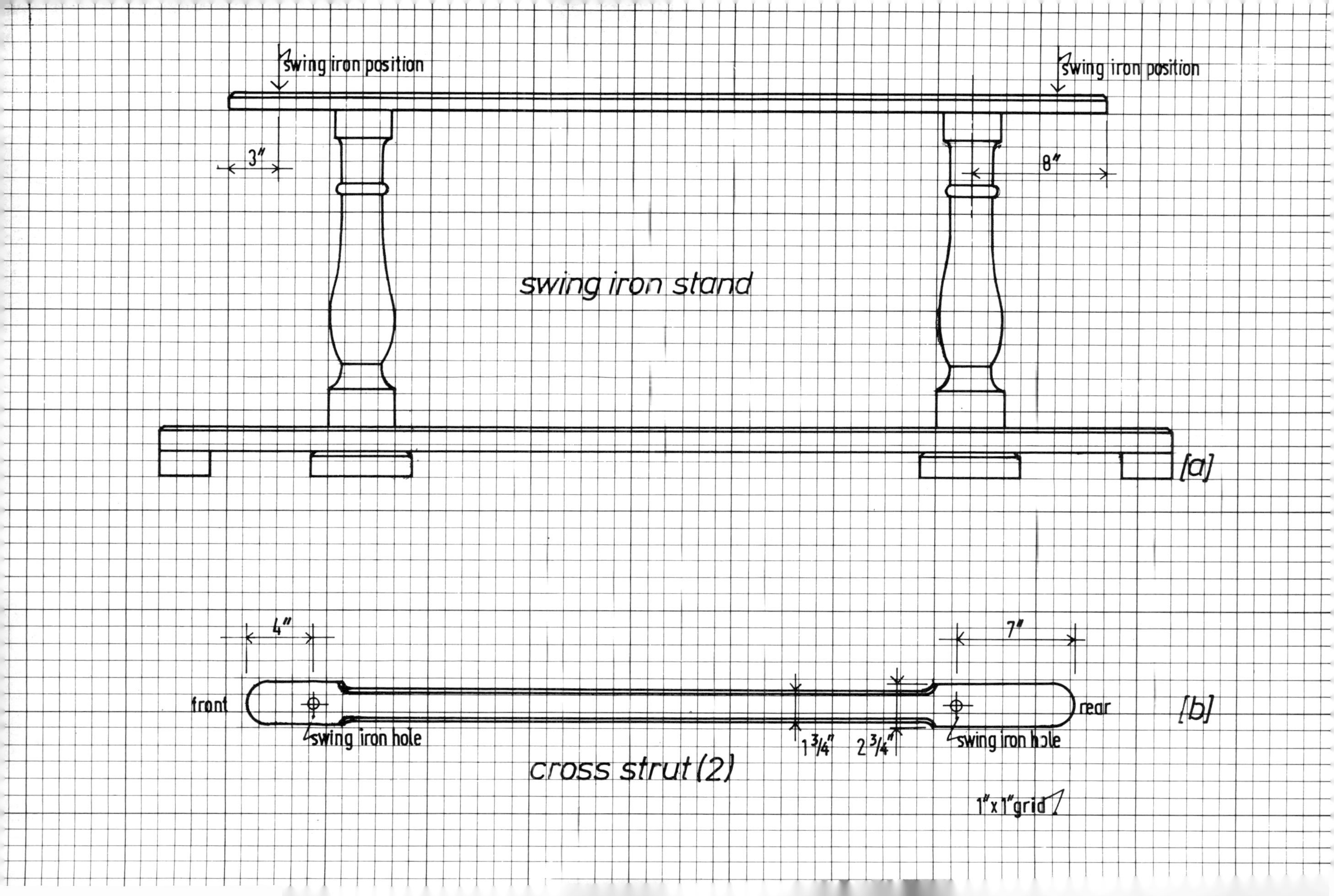
swing iron position
swing iron position
3"
8"
swing iron stand
[a]
4"
7"
front
swing iron hole
1 3/4"
2 3/4"
swing iron hole
rear
[b]
cross strut (2)
1"x1" grid

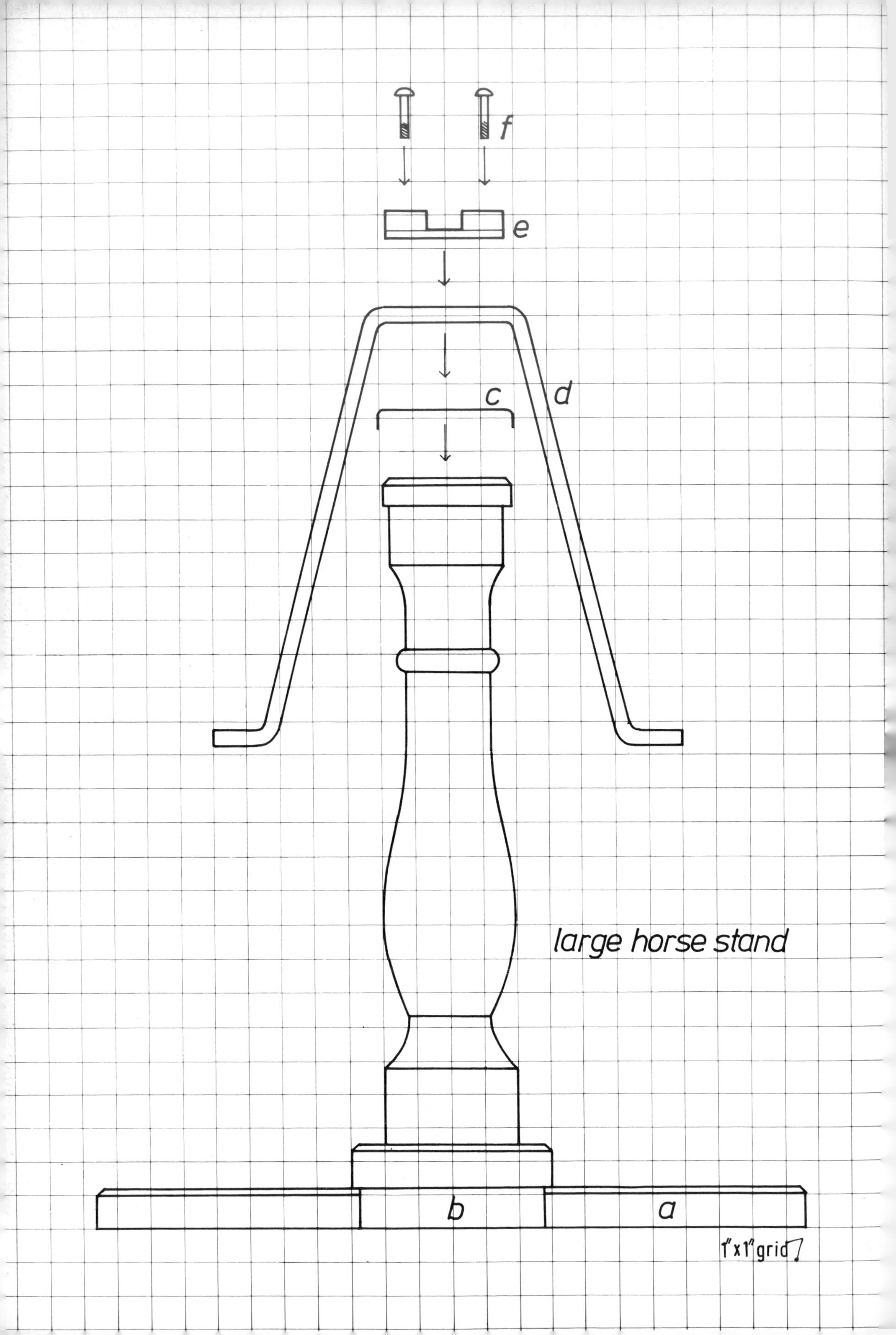

f
e
d
c
large horse stand
b
a
1"x1" grid

temporary cross struts (see page 71) and bolted onto the finished cross struts with their swing irons. Then a little grease is smeared on to the swing iron brackets and bearing strip and the horse lifted on to the stand and bolted in place (Plate 81). After the hooves have been touched up with black where the paint has been disturbed by the bolts, the horse is ready, at last, for its first rider (Plate 82).

Bow Rockers for the Small Horse (see scale drawings)

Bow rockers are made of ash and the two main curved rockers can be sawn from a single wide board which obviates the need for jointing in the middle (Plate 83). The waste cut from this board is used to make the rectangular frame in the middle around which the rockers are assembled, as well as the five pieces for the

Fig 26 Scale drawing of large horse stand, end view, showing: (a) cross piece which prevents the horse from tipping over sideways; (b) end piece which prevents the stand from tipping up endways; (c) steel bearing strip; (d) mild or bright steel rod swing iron; (e) swing iron bracket; (f) carriage bolts

Plate 80 Mild steel swing iron bracket

Plate 81 Detail of the hoof fixing to the cross strut, and brass 'bowler hat' which covers the end of the swing iron

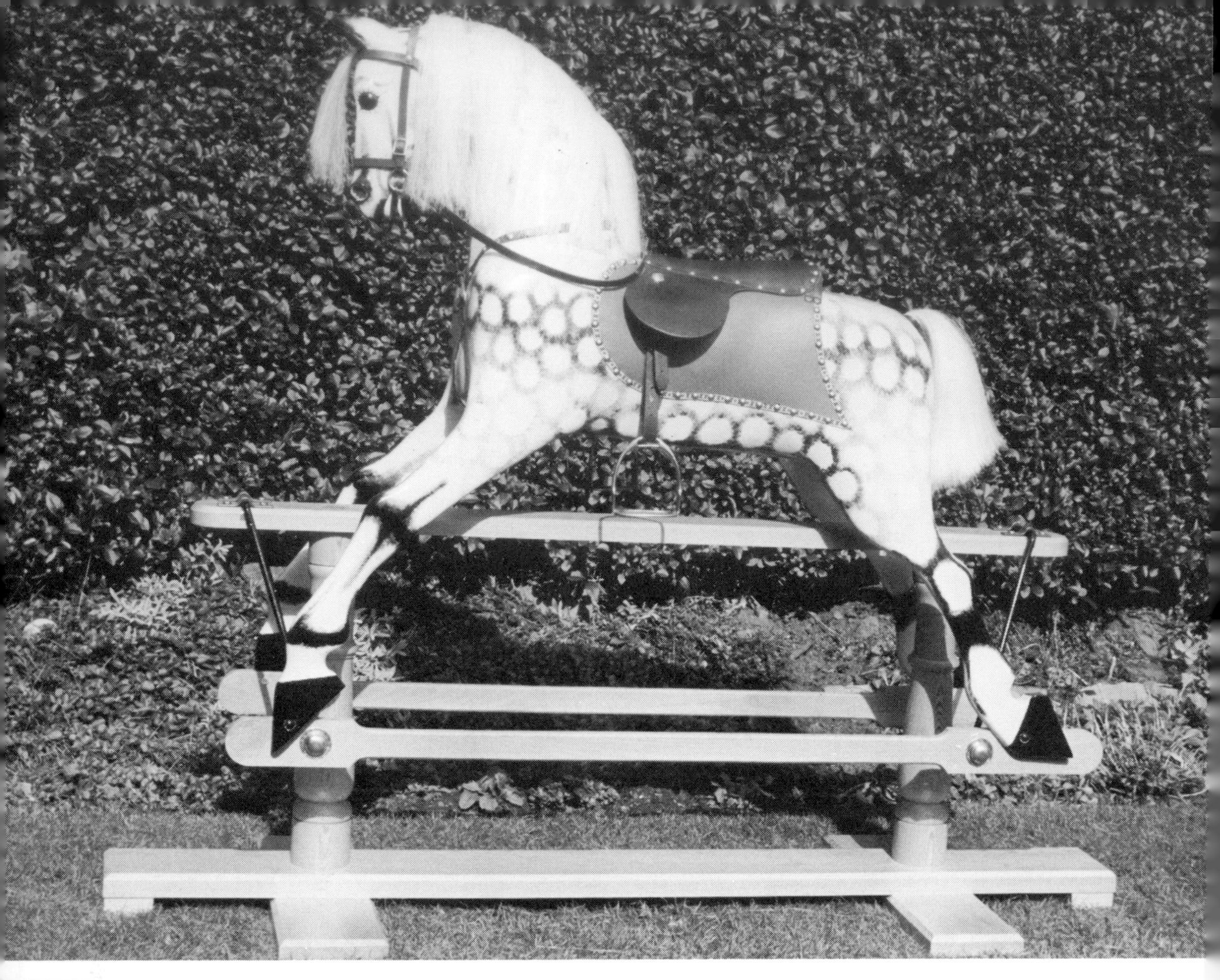

Plate 82 (above) The finished large rocking-horse awaiting its rider

Plate 83 (left) Band-sawing out the small horse ash rockers

slatted platform. The bows are angled inwards so that they are closer together at the ends than in the middle, giving the boat-shaped appearance. After the parts have been cut out the rectangular frame is assembled. The rockers are screwed onto this frame from the inside. It is as well to assemble the parts of the rockers without glue prior to gluing up to ensure that the various parts fit together sturdily.

At each end of the arrangement the rockers are connected together with a small piece of turned 2in x 2in (50mm x 50mm) ash. A piece 22in (560mm) long will be enough to turn both pieces together. It is best to mark out and par-

Fig 27 Large horse stand posts: (a), (b), (c) and (d) show designs for turned posts; (e) is a square section post tapered towards the top with square tenons cut to fit into mortices in the stand top and bottom

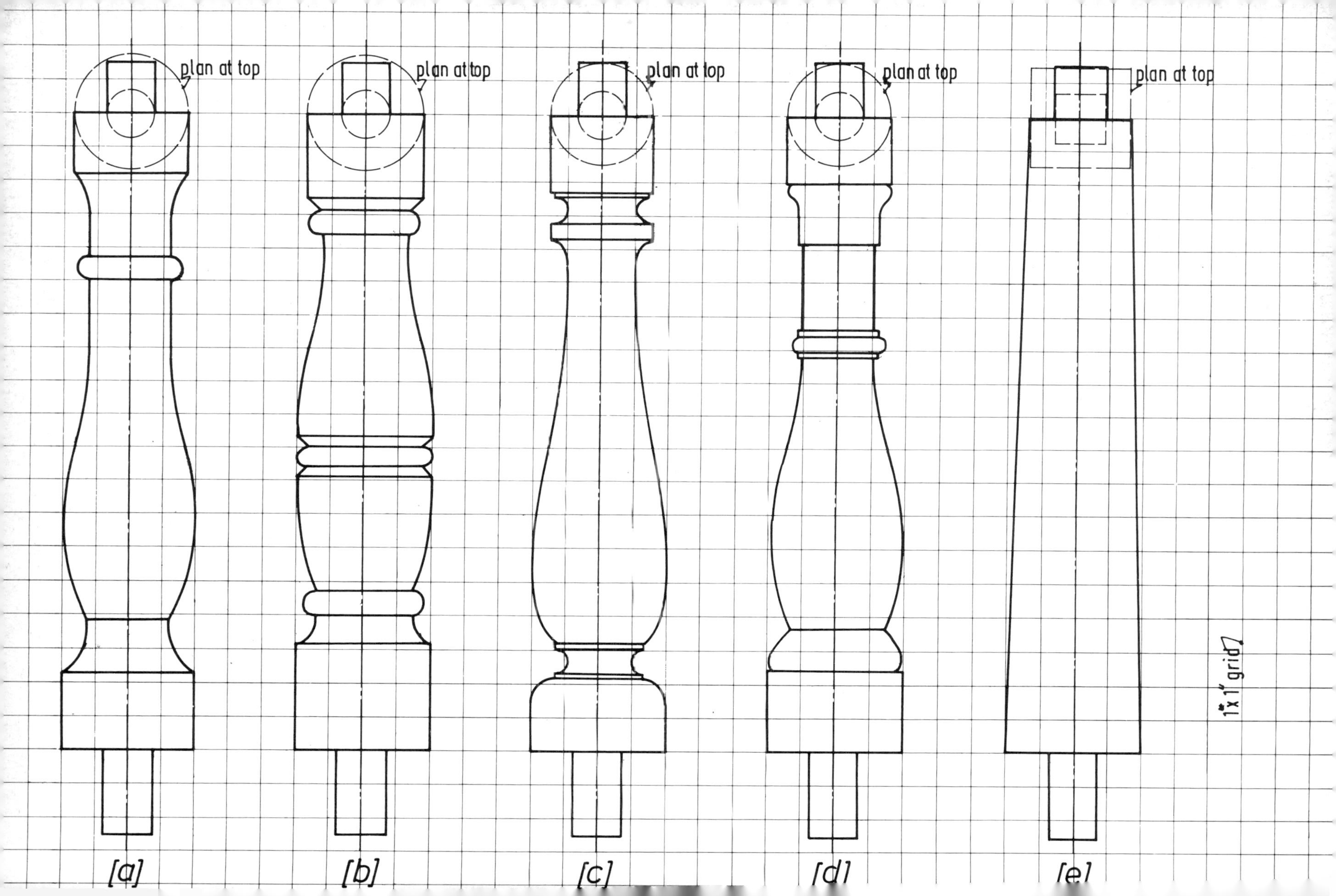
plan at top
plan at top
plan at top
plan at top
plan at top
[a]
[b]
[c]
[d]
[e]
1" x 1" grid

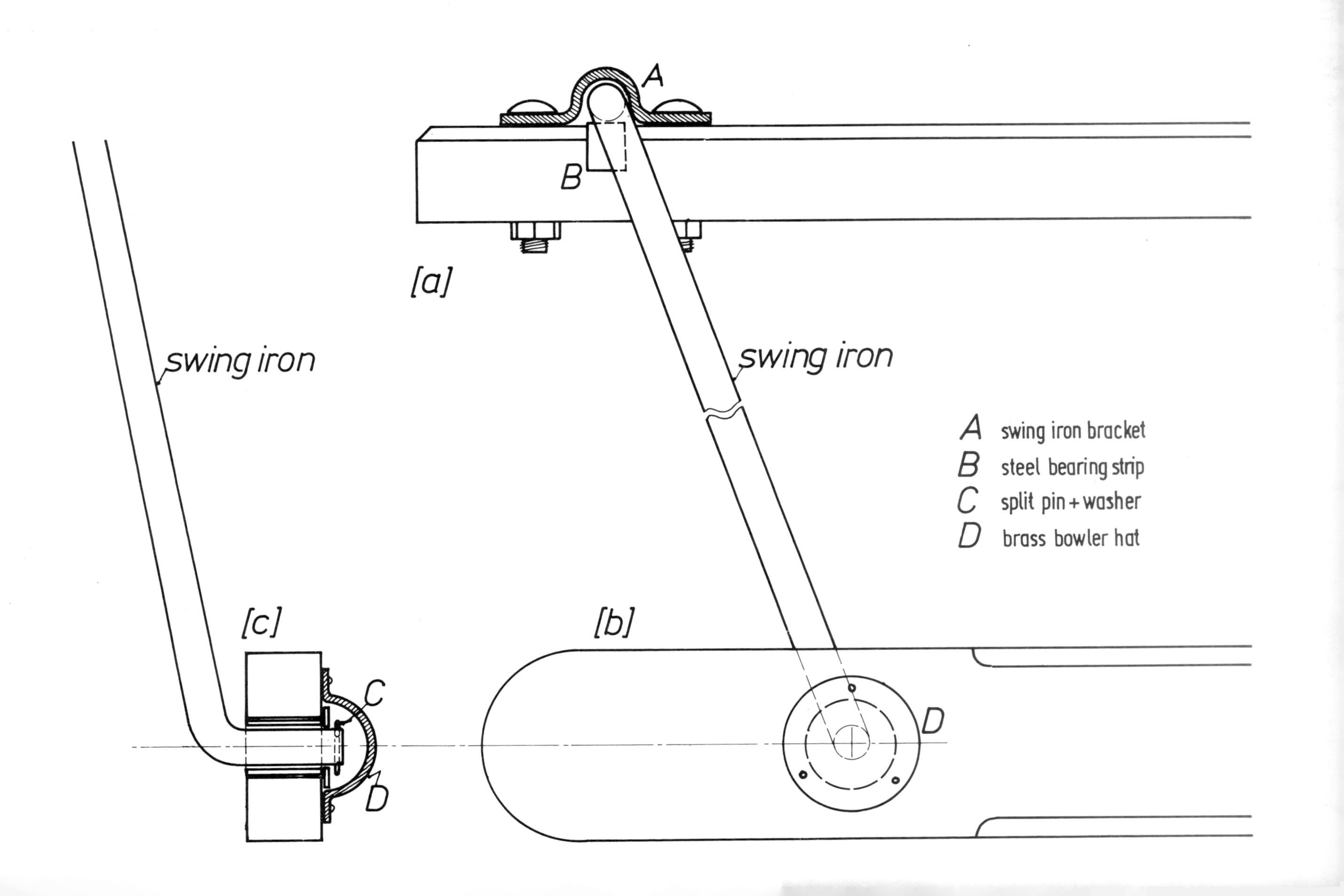
A
B
[a]
swing iron
swing iron
A swing iron bracket
B steel bearing strip
C split pin + washer
D brass bowler hat
[c]
C
D
[b]
D

tially saw the angles at each end of these pieces before putting the wood into the lathe (Plate 84). The ends of each piece are turned down to a suitable diameter to be pegged through holes of the same size, say 9/16in (15mm), in the main rockers. It is important to line these holes up as accurately as you can when drilling through (Plate 85). In the absence of a lathe, either square section timber or square chamfered down to octagonal section will be suitable, the ends being morticed into the rocker sides.

The upper and lower edges of the rockers are bevelled so that the upper edge is flat to take the slatted platform, the lower edge flat to the floor. A spokeshave is useful for this purpose. This bevelling should run out before the ends of the rockers, which remain square in section.

After a 'dry run' to check that everything fits (Plate 86), glue it all together. The middle frame and rockers are screwed together, the ends of the turned end pieces trimmed off and wedged in position. The five pieces of the slatted platform are chamfered round their upper edges and screwed in place (Plate 87). The rockers are varnished and polished, ash having a very pleasing appearance. The horse is fixed in place with a ¼in (6mm) carriage bolt at each hoof (Plate 88) and is ready to ride (Plate 89).

Fig 28 Large horse swing iron arrangement

Plate 84 Small horse rocker end pieces turned on the lathe. Note that the angled cuts have been partially sawn before putting the wood in the lathe — these will now be completed with a chisel

Plate 85 Assembling the small horse bow rockers

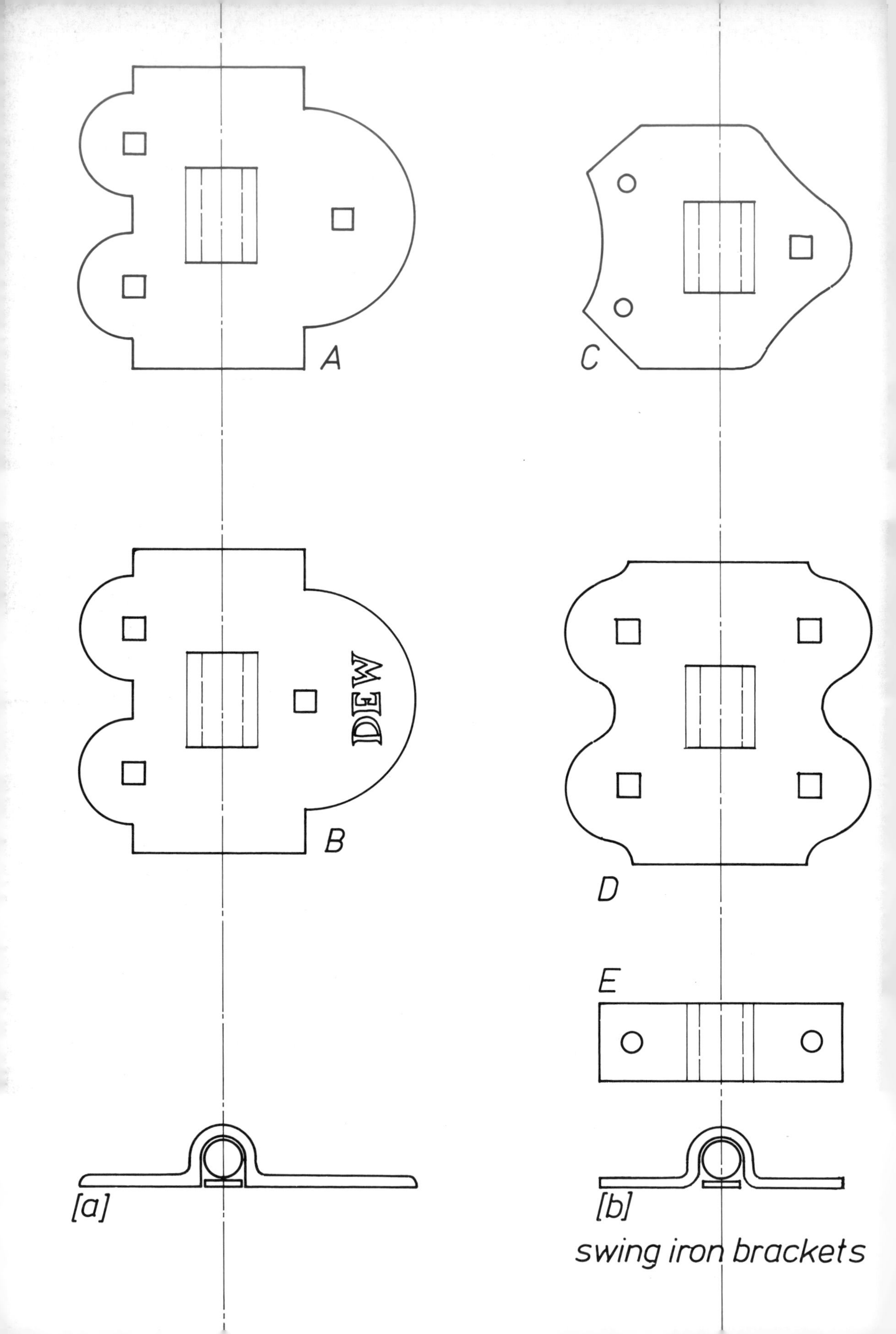

swing iron brackets

Plate 86 Dry assembly of the small horse bow rockers to check that all parts fit well

Fig 29 Swing iron brackets. A and B are cast in brass or bronze as fitted to the large horse in this book; (a) shows a side view with the swing iron resting on its steel bearing strip. C and D are often found on older horses and may be either cast or pressed. E is a simple pressed mild steel bracket which is used in pairs; (b) shows a side view of the pressed bracket with swing iron and bearing strip

Plate 87 Screwing on the slatted platform

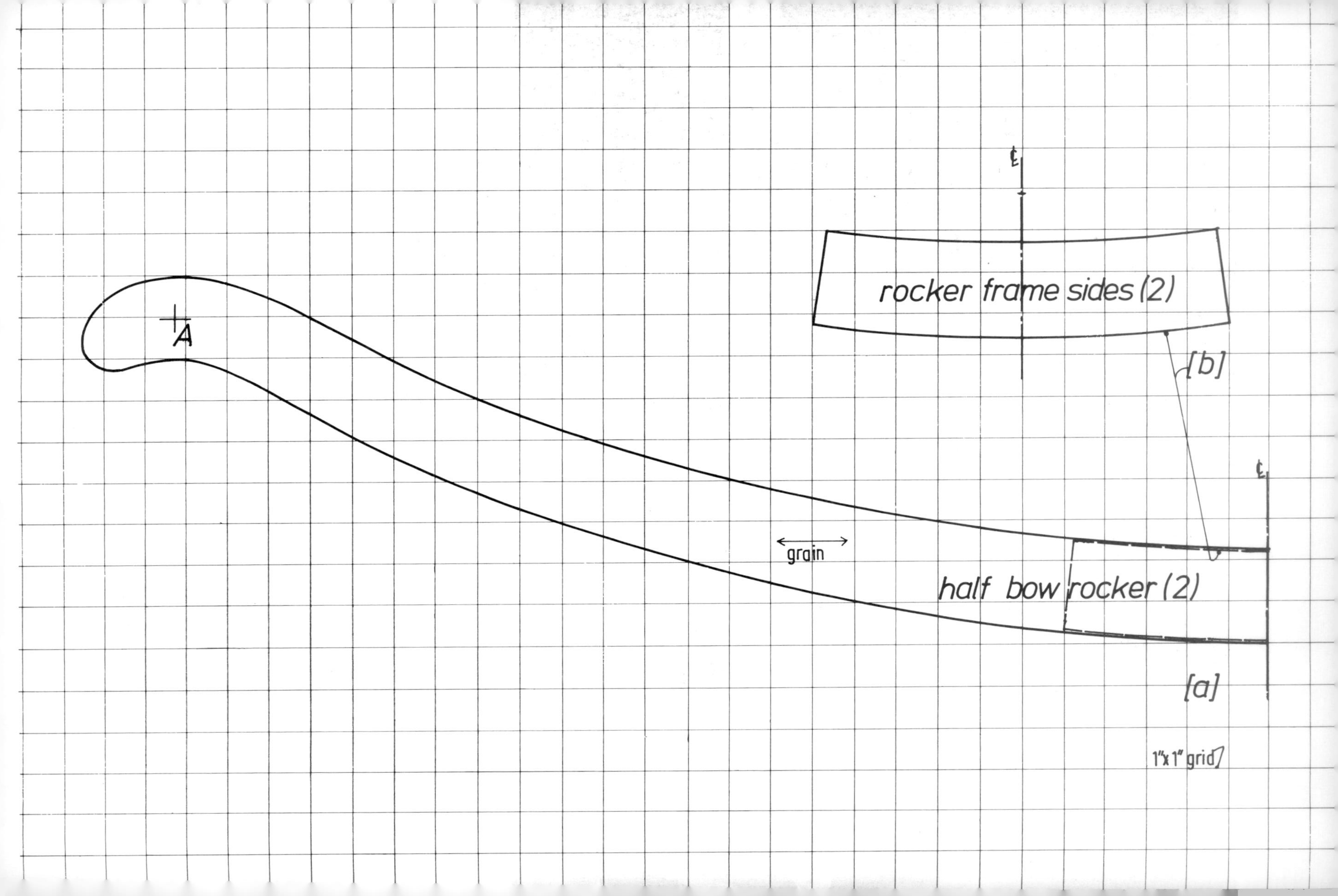
A
rocker frame sides (2)
[b]
grain
half bow rocker (2)
[a]
1"x1" grid

Plate 88 The small horse (in this case unpainted) mounted on its rockers after the hooves have been notched to fit neatly over the outer edge of the rockers. The horse is fixed to the rockers with either a wood screw or carriage bolt at each hoof

Fig 30 Scale drawing of small horse rocker showing (a) half of the curved bow rocker and (b) the rocker frame sides which together with the rocker base end pieces (shown in Fig 31) form the rectangular frame around which the rockers are assembled

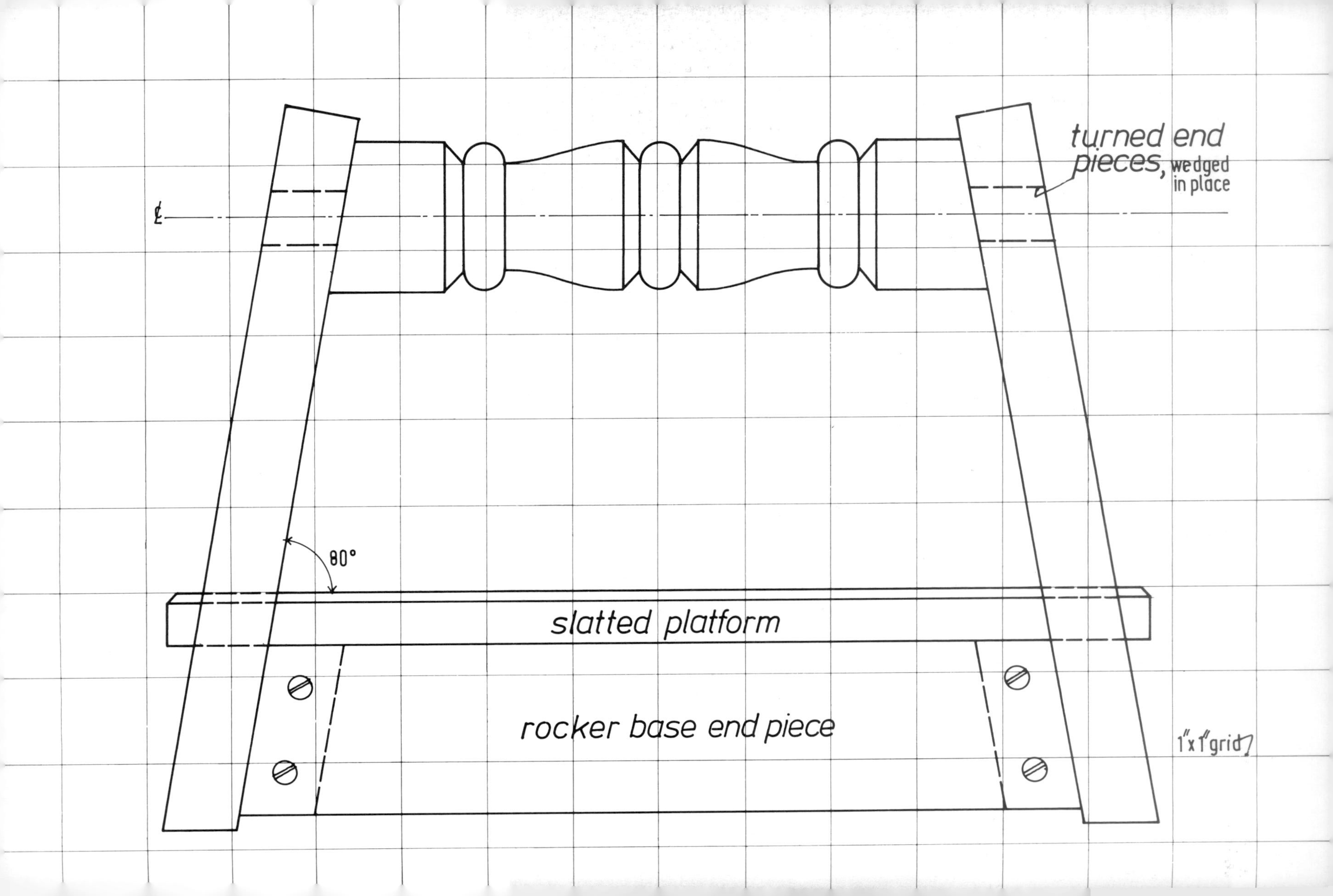
turned end pieces, wedged in place
80°
slatted platform
rocker base end piece
1"x1" grid

Plate 89 The small horse complete and mounted on its varnished ash rockers

Fig 31 Scale drawing of small horse rocker arrangement, end view

5
RENOVATING OLD ROCKING-HORSES

Imagine a brand new rocking-horse being taken from his maker's workshop, paintwork gleaming bright and fresh, mane and tail long, clean and flowing, a sparkle in his glass eye. He is welcomed rapturously into a family and the young children take eager turns to ride. He is too big to be put away like other toys but stands quietly in the corner ever ready for any interested child rider. Rocking to and fro, year in, year out, he grows old. His mane and tail are reduced to stubble. His once fine harness deteriorates and breaks; the stuffing falls out of his saddle. An ear is chipped and broken. The continual rocking wears grooves in the steel bearers and he becomes rickety and unstable. The children outgrow him and he is put aside into a storeroom or shed. Years pass; the children grow up and a new generation of babies comes along. The old rocking-horse is remembered. He is brought out again and dusted off. But how small and sad and shabby he is! He is sent off to the restorer. There he is completely stripped down; his broken ear is repaired; he is patched up and repainted, just like of old. The rickety stand is attended to and cleaned and he is remounted. He is given a new harness and saddle, new mane and tail. When the owners return to collect him they can hardly recognise him, but beneath the bright new paintwork and trimmings survives the same old horse, now as good as new again, ready to begin a whole new life bringing continuing pleasure to countless children.

One evening a lady telephoned to ask if I would restore an old wooden rocking-horse. It had been hers when she was a child and she had kept it stored away against the advent of her own children. Now the time had come to bring Dobbin out again for her young son. 'He's very dirty', she told me, 'but he is a lovely horse. I think he just needs a fresh coat of paint, and a new mane and tail and saddle.'

When I went along to collect the rocking-horse I found Dobbin languishing behind a pile of old carpets and junk in a garden shed. I leaned over to lift him out and . . . his head came off in my hand! 'I think', I said slowly, 'that this will require a little more than a fresh coat of paint.'

Wooden rocking-horses can and do stand

Plate 90 The result of long neglect in a damp shed

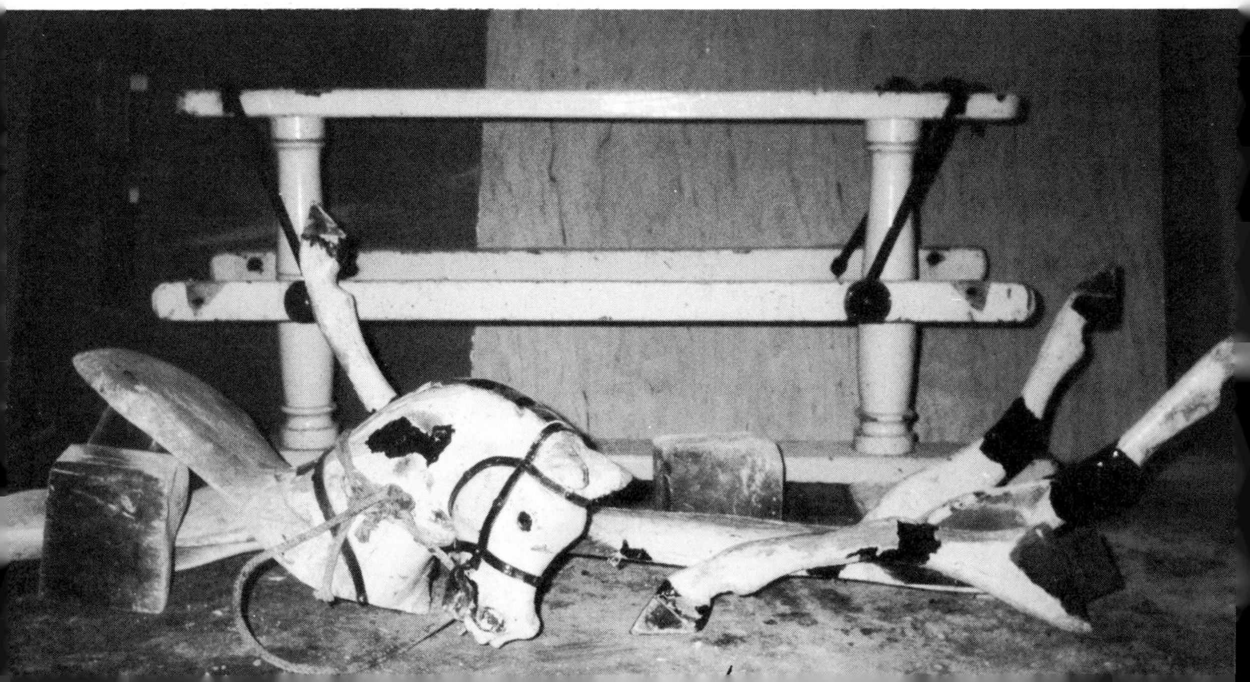

much abuse from children. (I once had one which appeared at first to have a terrible case of woodworm, until I realised it had been used as a target for darts practice.) But they cannot stand the rain. This one had been thoroughly rained upon — the leather had rotted and perished, the gesso was destroyed, and the glue in all the joints had disintegrated so that the horse fell apart into twenty or so wooden pieces, which I shoved into a sack.

The pieces needed a considerable period to thoroughly dry out, on the top shelf in my workshop, in the warmth. Several times I took the bits down, examined the dirty pile of firewood and then returned them to the top shelf. Eventually, however, I just had to get on with it.

I thoroughly cleaned off all the timber and glued it back together, splicing in new wood in a few places where the old was unusable or missing. It sprouted cramps and wedges like a strange Martian creature, but soon began to look like a wooden horse again. I applied new gesso, gave it a pair of new glass eyes, fresh dapple grey paintwork and a new harness, saddle, stirrups, mane and tail. I rebuilt the

Plate 91 The same rocking-horse as shown in Plate 90, re-built using nearly all the original timber

stand, stripped it to bare pine and varnished and polished it. The swing irons and brackets were de-rusted and painted afresh. Transformation! A new rocking-horse for an old one — but all (or nearly all) the original timber remained. I hope it serves its new child riders well.

I use the above story to illustrate my claim that no rocking-horse is so damaged as to be irreparable (or not worth while repairing). But of course the majority of old rocking-horses are nowhere near as bad as that. The usual problems are woodworm, broken ears, broken lower jaws, broken or loose legs, and general wear and tear.

If you are renovating an old horse the first job is to make the basic woodwork sound again and repair any broken bits. Once the woodwork is satisfactorily repaired the surface renovation can be completed with confidence.

The first job then, is to remove the horse from its stand (or rockers) by unscrewing the four securing bolts at each hoof. These usually

Plate 92 The same horse again — after the 'complete treatment'

come out fairly easily with a little persuasion from a hammer after loosening the nuts. Support the hoof by holding the palm of your hand over the head of the bolt and tap the loosened nut sharply. If these bolts do come out easily you can retain them to use again, but if they have rusted in place you may have to resort to pliers to wiggle them loose. Sometimes you can slip a thin hacksaw blade into the slight gap between hoof and cross strut and saw the bolt through, then tap out the broken bits with a hammer and nail punch. But do try to avoid damaging the wood surrounding the bolt hole. Also mark the cross struts 'front' and 'back' to remind you which way round the horse is mounted.

Using the bolt holes at each hoof, screw on a couple of laths of scrap wood, or, in the case of a horse on bow rockers, four pieces of scrap wood. These are to keep the hooves just above the floor or bench and enable you to move the horse around without risking chipping the tips of the hooves.

Next remove all the old tack — saddle, bridle, chest straps — and the remains of the old mane and tail. If possible retain the old saddle intact to use as a pattern for the new one. Nails should be removed as far as possible, or punched in. The nails along the back of the neck should be carefully removed, and, if there is no slot for the mane already, this can now be cut. The slot is approximately ¼in (6mm) wide and ½in (12mm) deep. It starts about an inch (25mm) or so behind the base of the ears and runs back along the middle of the neck for a distance appropriate to the size of the horse. The mane will be securely fixed in this slot, or on the surface of the neck.

Woodworm

Evidence of woodworm is quite common in the stand or rockers, less so in the gessoed and painted horse itself, though sometimes the worms spread from an infected stand through into the legs. This needs to be thoroughly treated with a commercial woodworm killer which is squirted into the holes. The holes are flight holes, indicating that the beetle has already flown away, but of course there may well be more larvae inside eating away at the wood, and these need to be killed to prevent further spread. If the worm has really severely attacked the wood to the point where the structural soundness of the timber is affected, it will be necessary to discard the affected timber and make a whole new stand, or leg or whatever. But usually, and if you are lucky, the damage will not be that severe. I always prefer to retain the original timber if possible, rather than renew it, but if there is any doubt about its soundness it had better be replaced.

Broken Ears and Jaw

Much the commonest repair required on an old wooden rocking-horse is to broken ears. This is of course because the ears are relatively thin, pointed, and they stick out; so they are vulnerable to knocks. Sometimes a rocking-horse head will have been cut from a piece of wood such that the grain runs across the ears and this unfortunate (in fact, bad) practice may have allowed the ears to snap off across the grain when knocked. The same applies to the lower jaw which is sometimes found to have broken off clean across the grain. If the head has been properly made, with the grain

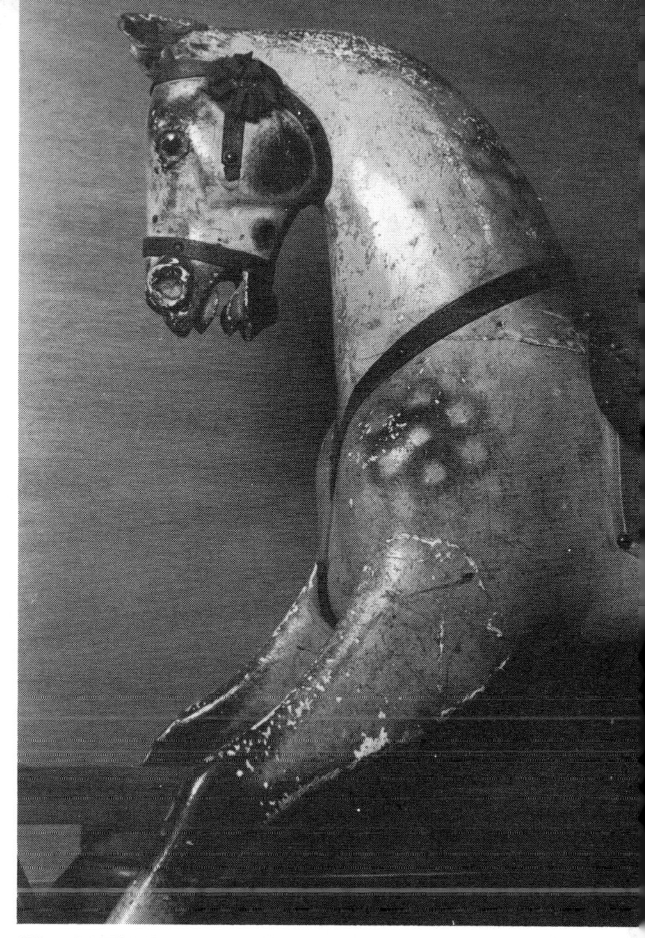

Plate 93 This horse shows the signs of normal wear and tear — a broken ear, cracked gesso, mane gone, harness disintegrated — but basically sound

Plate 94 The same horse after restoration and good for many more years

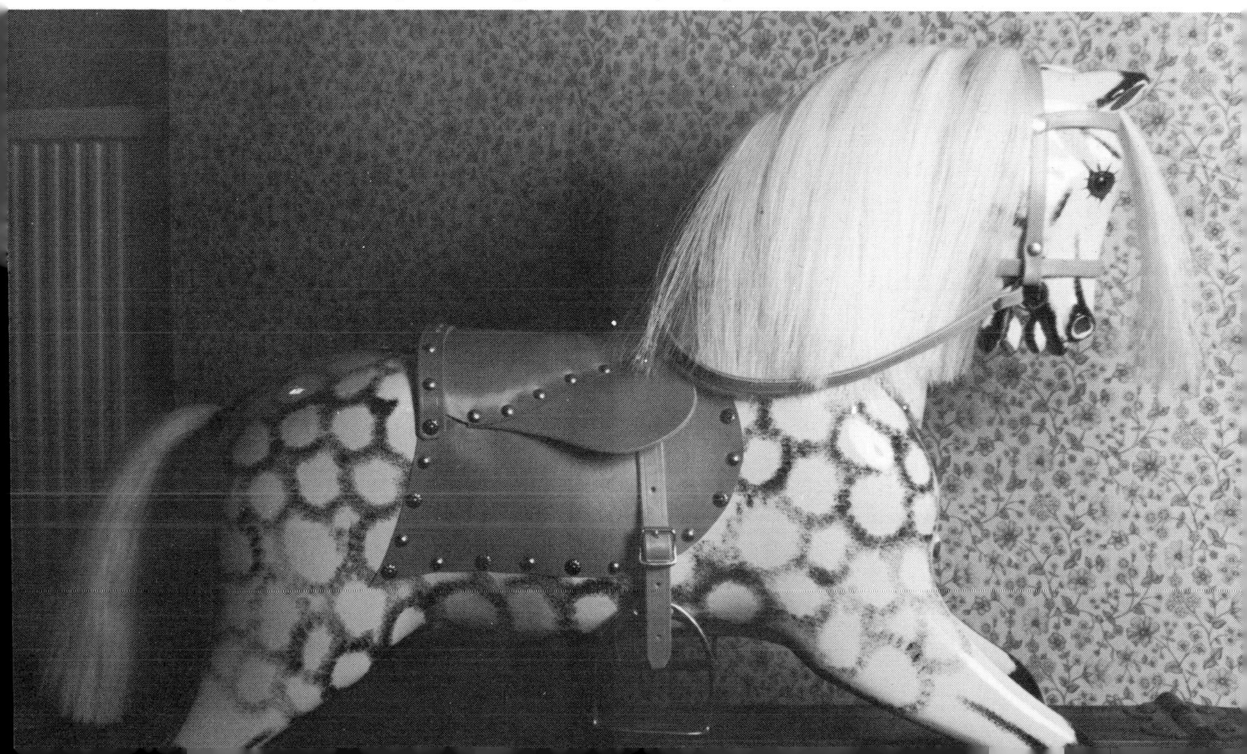

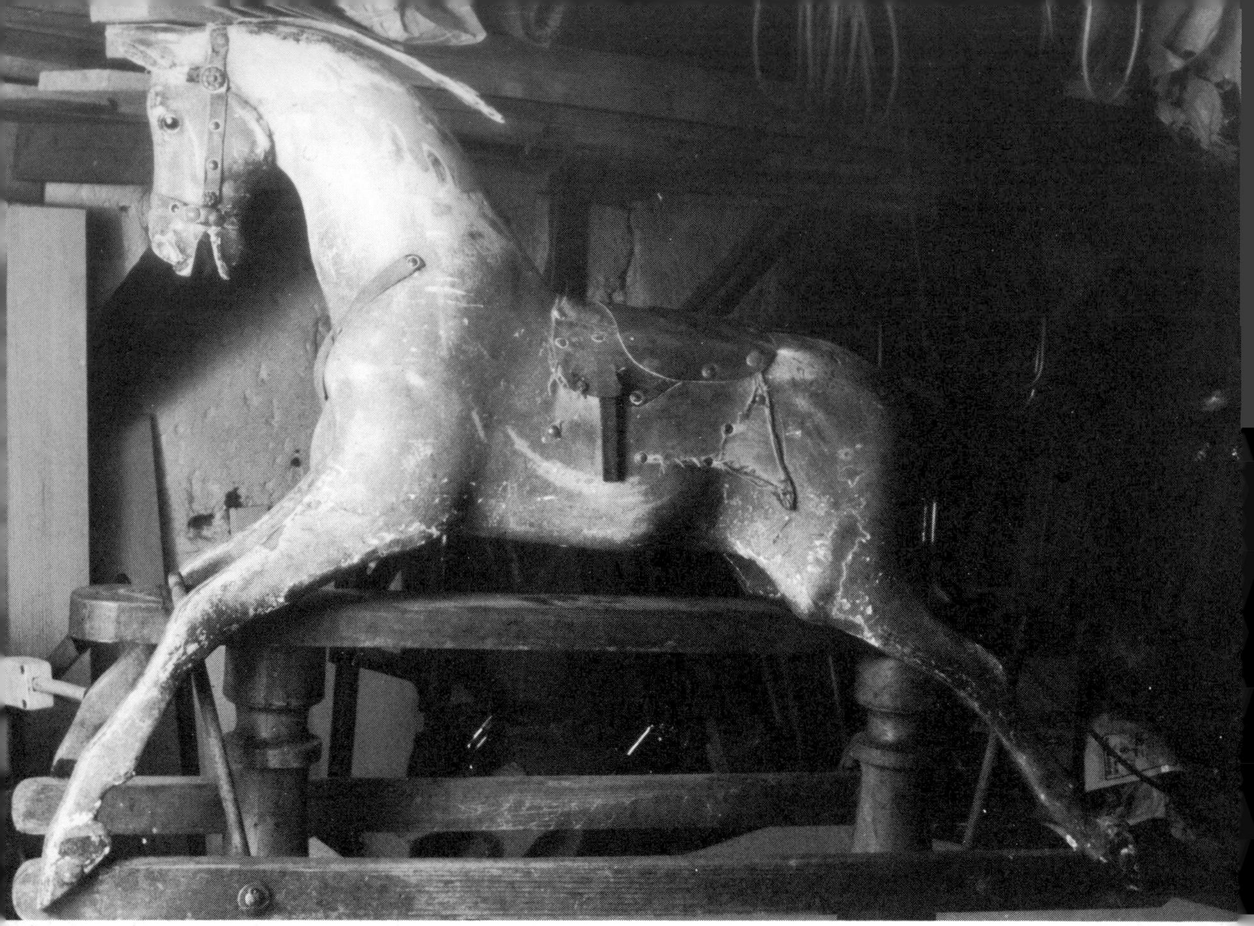

Plate 95 (above) This very attractive little horse, less than 3 feet (914mm) long, was built in 1905 and was originally painted as a palomino

Plate 96 (below) The same horse after restoration. The stand required treatment for woodworm, and the horse was painted a yellow ochre 'palomino' colour as near to the original colour as the author could mix, touched up with dabs of brown

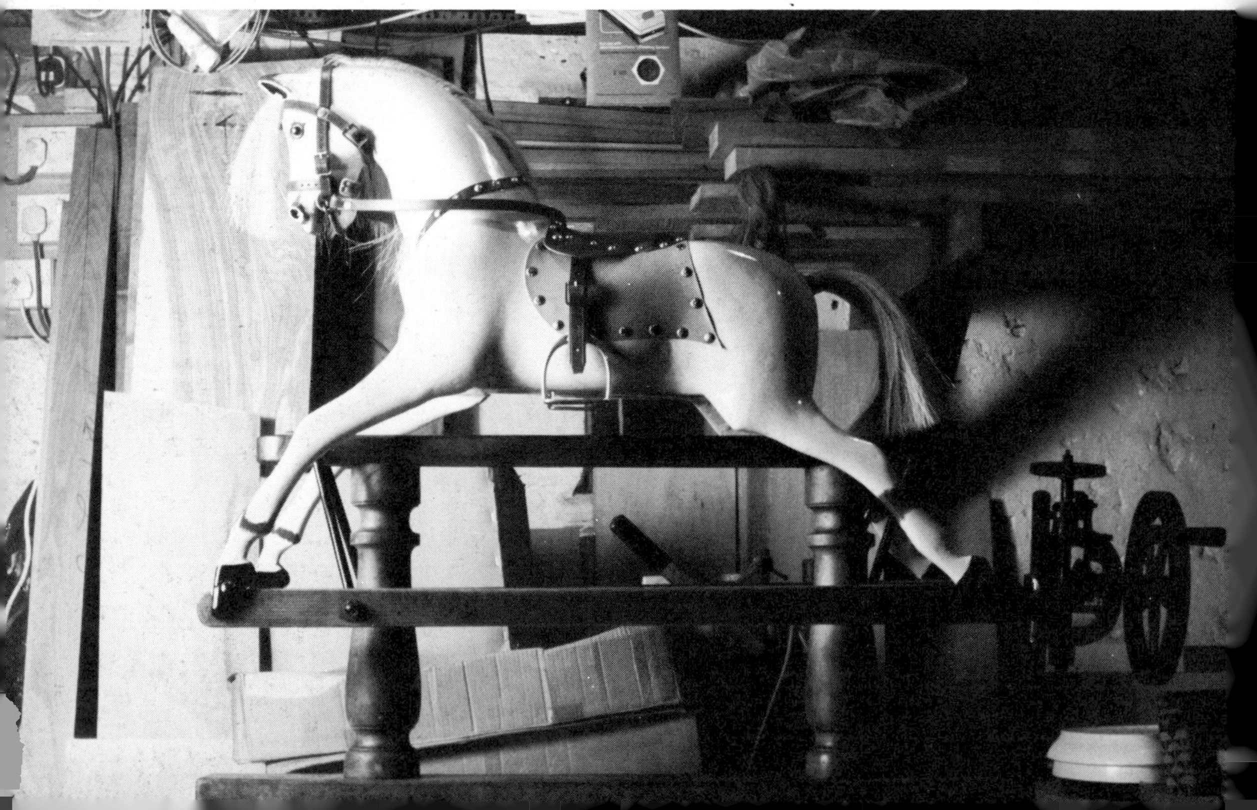

running more or less along the ears and jaw, any breakages due to knocks are more likely to be jagged and uneven.

Small breakages or chips off the ears can be repaired with small pieces of wood spliced and glued into the broken ear after first cutting it back to reveal clean wood. Then the new wood is carved in to match the old. Alternatively, body filler such as is used to repair dents in cars can be used to build up a slightly broken ear. This stuff sets extremely hard so it needs to be shaped and sanded down well before it finally hardens, which usually takes about twenty-four hours. It sticks quite well to wood so long as the surface is clean and keyed before application.

If the ears are badly broken (Plate 97) I prefer to cut them out altogether and carve in a new pair. Two saw cuts are made into the head of the old horse. The first runs horizontally back from a point immediately below the ears to meet the second saw cut which is made vertically just behind the ears and clear of the broken part. The two saw cuts meet as near to right angles as you can judge. Take a new piece of wood, which should be big enough to encompass the full width and length of the ears, and cut it so it fits snugly into the sawn right angle (Plate 98). Make it so the grain runs along the length of the proposed new ears. It is not a bad idea to use a harder wood than the original yellow pine — lime or sycamore for example. Then the new ears will be much stronger than the old.

With a band- or coping saw cut out the rough shape of the new ears and drill for a screw hole which runs in at an angle between the ears towards the corner of the right angle. The piece can then be glued and screwed in place. The screw head should be set well into the wood to allow for further carving. The screw hole can be filled later. When the glue is set the ears can be finally carved to shape (Plate 99), keeping the old broken ears to hand so you can

Plate 97 This rocking-horse's ears were badly broken, along with general wear and tear over the rest of the horse and stand

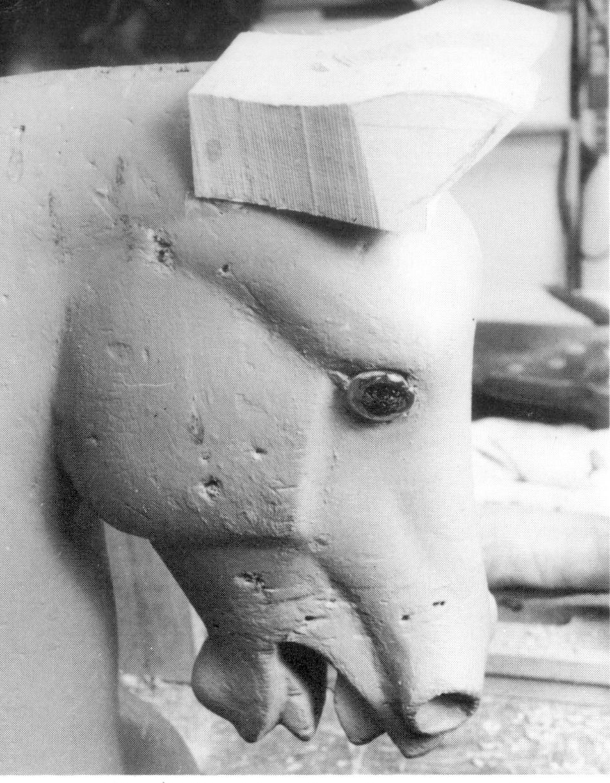

Plate 98 The old ears have been cut out and a new block, rough shaped, has been glued and screwed in position

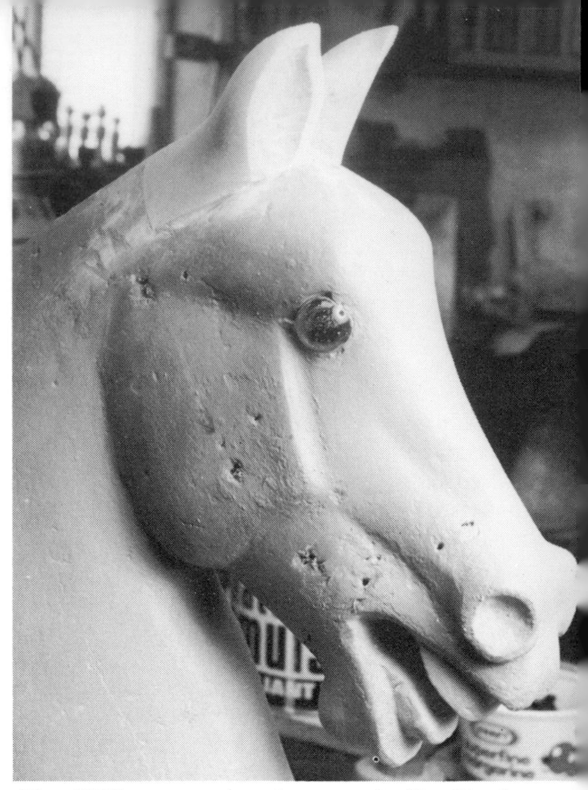

Plate 99 The new ears have been carved to blend in; the holes and blemishes will be filled before painting over

Plate 100 The finished horse after restoration. Part of the stand had to be renewed as it was badly broken; the stand was finally painted red

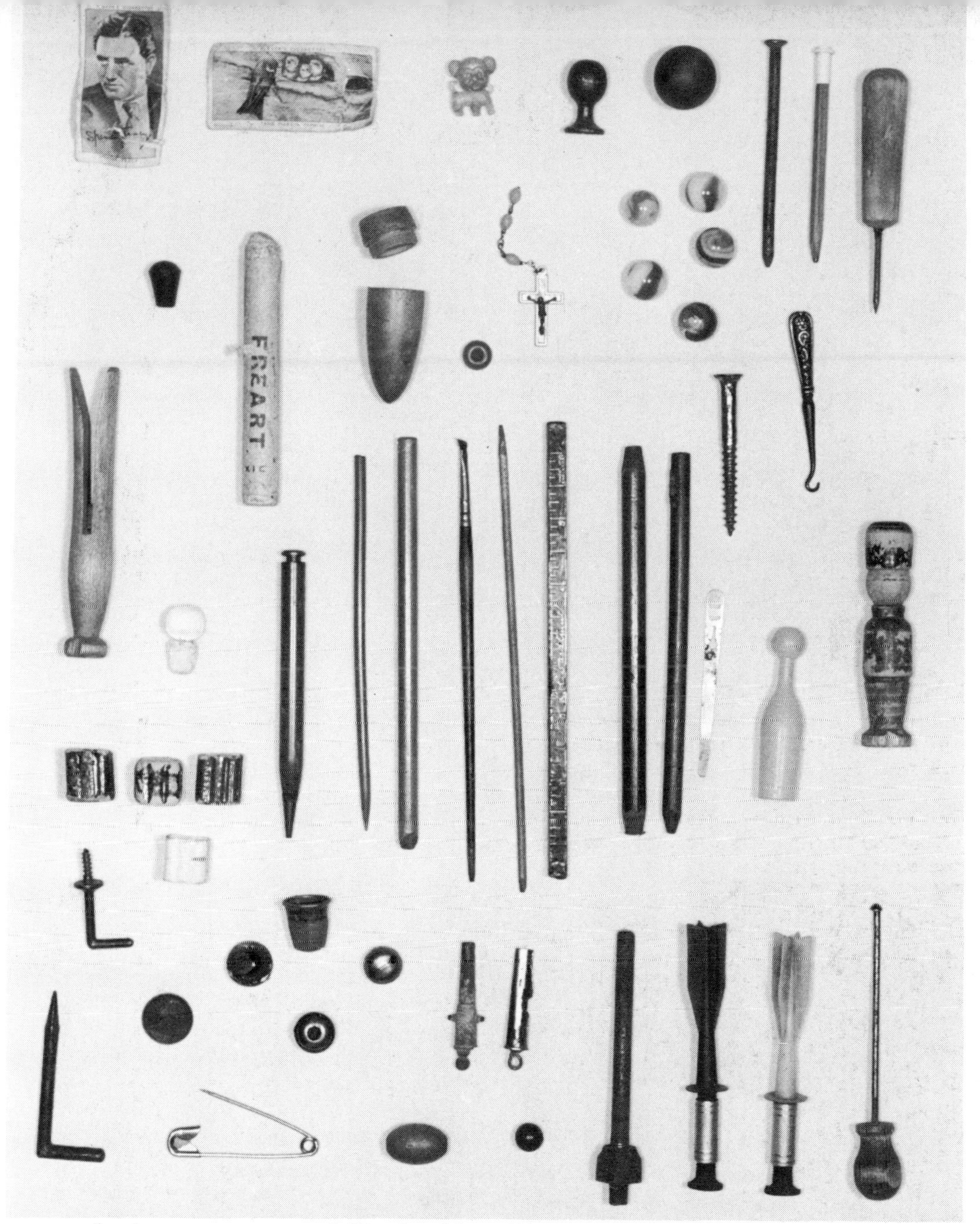

Plate 101 A selection of some of the objects found inside old rocking-horses. When the old tail has fallen out, children will poke small objects through the hole — along with dozens of pencils and marbles, the author has found a sandalwood needlecase, cigarette cards, a toy lead cannon, a Victorian boot hook, pegs, wooden soldiers, thimbles, darts, jacks and various unidentifiable 'mystery objects'

try to make the new ones as much like the old ones would have been originally by imagining the shape they were and cutting into the wood accordingly.

Broken lower jaws can be replaced in the same way, gluing and screwing a rough shaped block up onto a prepared flat surface cut across above the break and then carving the block into the desired shape. In this case there will not normally be any broken piece to guide the carving but a satisfactory repair can be accomplished without too much difficulty. It sounds much harder than it is. A good look at the ears and jaw of an unbroken wooden rocking-horse will indicate the sort of shapes that are suitable.

Plate 102 This horse's broken leg was removed from its mortice

Plate 103 A new beech leg was cut to fit

Plate 104 The small muscle block was fitted at the top of the leg and carved to match in with the body

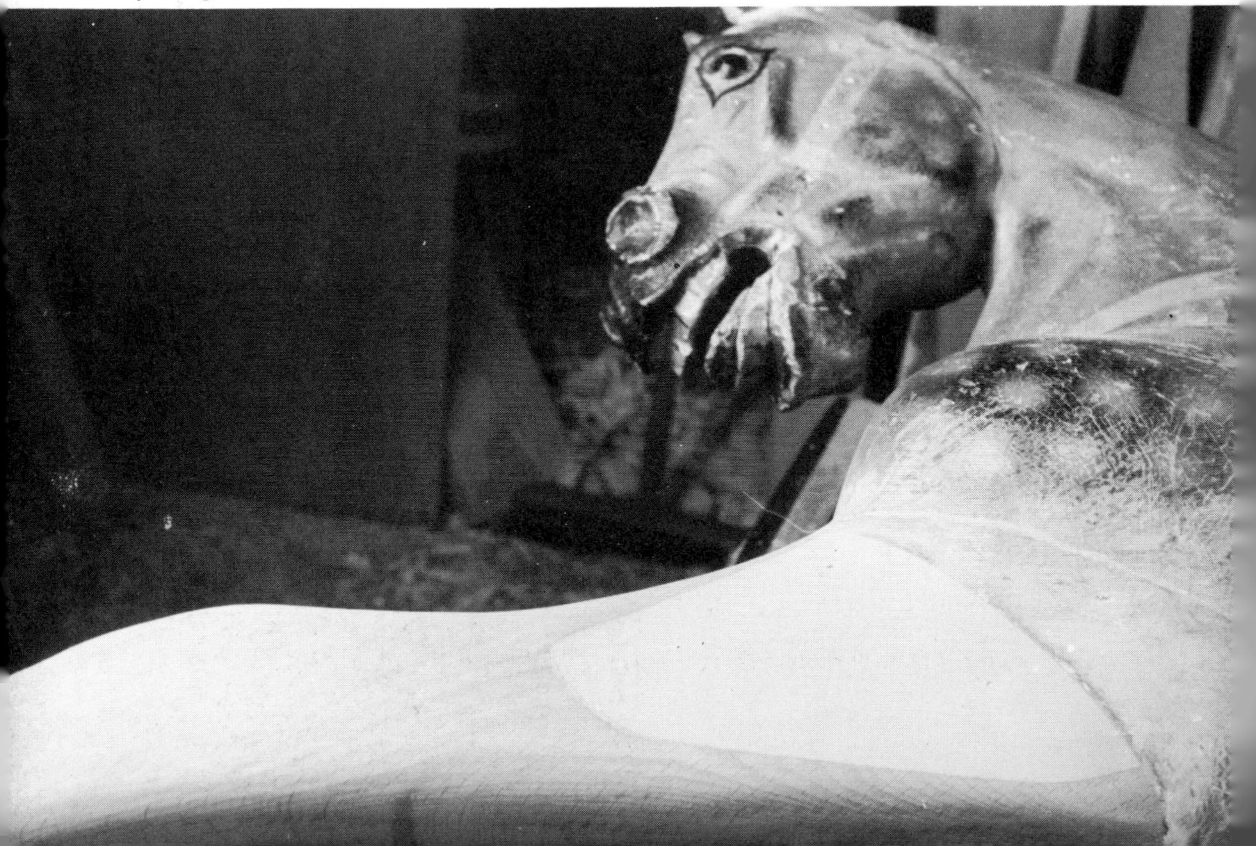

Loose or Broken Legs

The legs of most old rocking-horses are morticed into the body and were not always a particularly good fit even when new. So if they have worked loose it is as well to persuade them out altogether, perhaps with the aid of heat from a steam kettle, being careful not to melt the glue on adjacent joints. You will probably have to remove the small shaped muscle blocks at the top of each leg to do this, and you may find the leg joint has also been nailed through, so the nail will have to be removed. Then the leg can be cleaned off and replaced using a glue with some gap filling properties (urea formaldehyde) or by resetting the leg into its mortice slot with polyester resin. Removing and replacing the leg without breaking the wood can be tricky; almost certainly the muscle blocks will break and need to be replaced with new wood. It is worth taking some trouble over loose legs, however, because the slightest movement will soon crack the new paintwork you will shortly be applying.

If a leg is badly broken or damaged a whole new leg may have to be made and fitted (Plate 102). I regularly receive for renovation a particular make of wooden rocking-horse in which softwood is often used for the legs. On a couple of occasions I have found that where the hoof fixing bolt has worked loose the bolt hole through the softwood hoof has become so worn and enlarged with use that the whole leg has had to be renewed. Sometimes even the better beech legs get broken and have to be renewed. In this case remove the old leg carefully so that is can be used as a pattern for the new one. Cut the tenon first, and if the old leg is completely broken make a cardboard pattern of the tenon to fit into the mortice to enable you to judge the correct angle. The tenon needs to be cut carefully and made to fit tightly (Plate 103). The rest of the leg is then rough shaped and glued in place. The muscle block is glued on top and the finishing carving done after the glue has set (Plate 104); you will have the corresponding leg on the other side to refer to in order to get the new leg to match the old (Plates 105 and 106).

Although some old rocking-horses are very well carved and constructed, many, particularly 'between-the-wars' factory-built rocking-

Plate 105 Front view of the same horse after renovation

Plate 106 Detail of the head — note that this horse has a tongue

horses, are surprisingly crudely shaped. You may well for example find areas where rough saw marks are still in evidence; the body blocks and muscle blocks may be nailed on as well as glued. Even if you do not possess much expertise at woodwork there is no need to be frightened off tackling repairs. The best of the old rocking-horse makers could achieve a delightful, vital, and wholly satisfactory result quickly and competently with a few deft and skilful strokes of saw and gouge. But what the amateur lacks in skill and experience he can, to a large degree, compensate for by taking time and care with his work.

Paintwork

Once any woodworm has been treated and repairs to the woodwork are complete, the whole surface of the horse needs to be rendered fit to receive the paintwork. Traditionally, rocking-horses have a brightly painted finish — in particular the dapple grey in which Victorian and Edwardian rocking-horses were almost invariably painted. But though this was the characteristic, it was by no means the only paint finish given to old rocking-horses. There are plain brown or black ones, and yellowish-brown palominoes, usually with contrasting 'socks' and head blaze. In my renovation work I normally try to restore the horse to something very like its original appearance. The original colouring is usually discernable and a reasonable match can be made by mixing paints. Not changing it too much is part of continuing the 'life' of a particular rocking-horse; but you may, if you so wish, paint a rocking-horse any colour under the sun, or not at all. I have seen an old rocking-horse which had been completely stripped of its paint and gesso, down to the bare yellow pine, then smoothed, varnished and polished. The underlying timber was in particularly good condition and it looked most impressive — as an artefact. As a toy for children though, I felt it had lost its character and joyfulness.

To receive paint then, the surface needs to be sanded smooth and blemishes filled. If the gesso is in very poor condition you may feel you would like to re-gesso the whole horse, in which case all the old gesso should be removed with a yacht scraper and coarse glasspaper. Gessoing, for those who wish to try it, is described in Appendix 2. Many people prefer to simply fill any blemishes with some commercial filler, sand smooth and repaint. The method of applying dappling in the traditional manner is described in Chapter 4.

The following alternative dappling methods may be attempted. Cut a number of discs of stiff paper, about 1½in–2in (40mm–50mm) in diameter. Stick them onto the horse's body and neck with double-sided masking tape or 'Blu-tack'. Then lightly spray on black gloss paint, holding the nozzle at least 9in (230mm) away from the surface. When the discs are removed (after the paint has dried) the effect is not unlike that achieved with the dappling pads — though a spray is more difficult to control and details of the facial features are hard to delineate. A test piece should be tried out first on a scrap of grey painted wood. An air brush could well be used to good effect. You can also use a stencil brush — a round, fat brush with short stiff hairs. The brush is kept almost dry and the black paint applied sparingly in a dabbing motion. A little white paint may also be used to highlight some areas. Avoid using too much paint or the effect may become messy or fussy; try out the dappling on a test piece first.

The Stand

While the paint is drying on the horse turn your attention to the stand. I shall be speaking of swing iron safety stands here, because these are so much more common, but some of the comments will apply equally to bow shaped curved rockers. Stands were commonly varnished though cheaper rocking-horses may have had painted stands from new. If a stand retains its original varnish it may simply require cleaning up, which can be done with a mixture of white spirit (turpentine), linseed oil and vinegar rubbed in with a cloth or fine wire wool, and then wax polished. If it has been painted, scrape off the old paint with the help of a commercial paint stripper. Sometimes you will find good looking timber beneath the paint which can be thoroughly cleaned, varnished and polished to good effect. A number of different woods were used for making the stand; I have found stands made from yellow pine, paraná pine, pitch pine, Douglas fir, oak and beech etc; the posts were often made of oak, beech or elm. Bow rockers are usually ash. Sometimes you will find the wood, although sound, is of such poor appearance that it needs to be hidden beneath a new coat of paint rather than varnished, though a black varnish might be used to mask ugly or ill-matching timbers.

It may be that the stand has become rickety through loosened joints, or even broken, so that woodwork repairs are called for. I try to retain as much of the original timber as possible but if a part is badly broken it may have to be replaced. Occasionally it may be necessary to build a whole new stand (see Chapter 4). On cheap rocking-horses the stand posts may be merely glued and nailed in place. But usually the lower ends of the stand posts are wood-screw threaded to screw into the stand bottom, the upper peg being wedged in place. If the posts are loose, drill out the top wedges and knock off the top of the stand by tapping upwards with a mallet. Then unscrew the posts, clean the threads and glue back in place, adding a wedge or two from the bottom for extra security. If the threads are badly damaged it may be necessary to saw off the lower peg of the stand post, drill out a hole up into the stand post, turn a piece of suitable wood to fit the hole and glue back together, wedging at both ends.

The cross struts can be stripped and varnished or painted to match the stand. The metal fittings — swing irons, brackets etc — should be cleaned off, primed and repainted. And just one last thing on the stand. Beneath the swing iron brackets are usually strips of steel for the swing irons to bear upon. These are invariably badly worn and need to be replaced with new strips of steel of appropriate size, which are nailed or screwed in place. Add a dab of grease before bolting back the brackets.

Finishing

Although most old rocking-horses have the bridle nailed in place I always make a small bridle out of good quality leather with little buckles, like a tiny version of a real bridle, which children can unbuckle and take off. It has a small bit forged out of mild steel with brass harness rings. Apart from the fact that this is a nice thing for children to play with, it avoids having to bang more nails into an old horse's wooden head.

The stirrups can either hang on straps through giant staples in the horse's sides, or onto a strap hung over the horse's back, fixed beneath the saddle in the centre (as described for the large and small horses respectively in Chapter 4). Saddlecloths, usually of leathercloth, are fixed each side, providing a splash of bright colour, then the saddle flaps, sponge padding and saddle top are added (see Chapter 4 for details). If the original saddle has been retained intact this can be used as a pattern for cutting the various parts of the new saddle.

On many older horses you may find two holes ¾in (19mm) or so in diameter, one either side of the horse's back just above the stirrup staples; a lot of people are puzzled by these. Originally they housed the lower ends of thick steel rods which curved out and up, or wooden pegs. These were usually covered in leather and served to provide a secure seat for tiny children who would hook their legs over them. They came out through holes cut in the saddle flaps which, when the pommels were not in use, were covered by small shaped flaps of leather. These leg supports are usually missing, leaving only the evidence of the holes. But few parents these days would want to place a very tiny child on a rocking-horse and leave him or her unattended; and as soon as a child is old enough to maintain balance unaided these supports are no longer needed. I do not normally attempt to replace them — the holes are simply left, out of sight beneath the saddle flaps.

The saddle is nailed in place so that there is no possibility of it moving or slipping when being ridden. Position the pieces first with 1in (25mm) round wire nails, the heads of which are later hidden beneath the heads of brass dome nails, or fancy-headed nails placed at intervals of about 1–1½in (25–40mm) around the edges, and also along the chest straps. Chest straps are fixed to converge at the middle of the chest and at this point a rosette can be placed.

The mane and tail are secured as described in Chapter 4, and the tail strap fixed. Finally, the horse is re-mounted on its stand and is, at last, ready for its child rider. A thing of beauty: a joy . . . until at last it gets so worn and battered it needs to return again for another exercise in revitalisation. Would that we humans could anticipate such immortality.

SAVE THE
WOODEN ROCKING-HORSE

APPENDIX 1

Conversion Table for Scale Drawings

The scale drawings in this book are based on a 1in grid. For those people who wish to use the metric measurements given in the text, the scale drawing measurements should be converted as follows:

in	*mm*	*in*	*mm*
⅛	3.2	1	25.4
¼	6.4	2	50.8
⅜	9.5	3	76.2
½	12.7	4	101.6
⅝	15.9	5	127.0
¾	19.1	10	254.0
⅞	22.2	20	308.0

APPENDIX 2

Gesso

Gesso, a mixture of animal glue and whiting, can be difficult to apply satisfactorily without a little practice, but the following should provide a useful guide to the method of mixing and application. All the ingredients for gesso can be obtained from suppliers of artists' materials.

Rabbit skin glue is obtainable either already broken into small pieces, or in sheet or slab form which should be broken up by being wrapped in a clean cloth and pounded with a mallet. The glue is then soaked in cold water overnight; 3¼oz (80g) of rabbit skin glue will make about 2 pints of size (thin glue). It swells to about three times its own volume and any unswollen lumps should be removed.

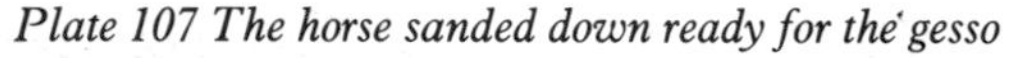

Plate 107 The horse sanded down ready for the gesso

The size is heated in a glue kettle (a ceramic jar or Pyrex bowl in a saucepan of water over the heat will serve). It should be as hot as possible but must not boil. Allow it to cool to room temperature when it should assume the texture of a firm, but not tough, jelly. To test it, press with two fingers, spreading them so that the jelly cracks apart. The sides of the crack should look rough or granular; if they are smooth the size is too strong and a little more water should be added. In any case, as you use the size you will lose some water through evaporation and it may be necessary to add a drop of water from time to time to keep the consistency correct. This is important because if the size is too concentrated the surface of the gesso will dry too hard and crack. On the other hand if it is too diluted the surface will be too soft and will clog the abrasive paper. Over-dilution can be rectified by adding a few pieces of glue soaked in very little water.

To apply the gesso it is best to use a wide flat brush. Heat the size up again in the glue kettle and give the horse a preliminary coat of size only (Plate 108). Then mix in sufficient gilder's whiting to produce a thin, smooth cream, stirring gently to avoid making air bubbles. The hot gesso should then run smoothly off the brush without drips or lumps. It is best to further smooth the gesso by straining it through a fine sieve or cheesecloth.

Keep the gesso hot (but not boiling) throughout. Apply quickly with light strokes

Plate 108 (opposite top left) A coat of size is brushed on first, then the whiting is added to make gesso

Plate 109 (opposite top right) Scrim is laid over the joints during the application of the first coat

Plate 110 (opposite bottom left) Building up the gesso — laying successive coats quickly on top — to seven or more coats

Plate 111 (opposite bottom right) The gesso complete

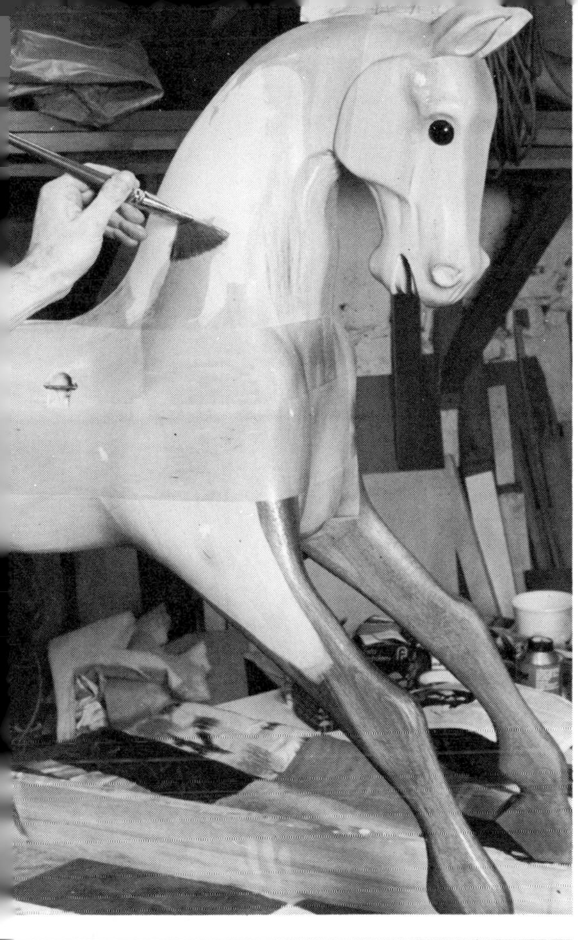

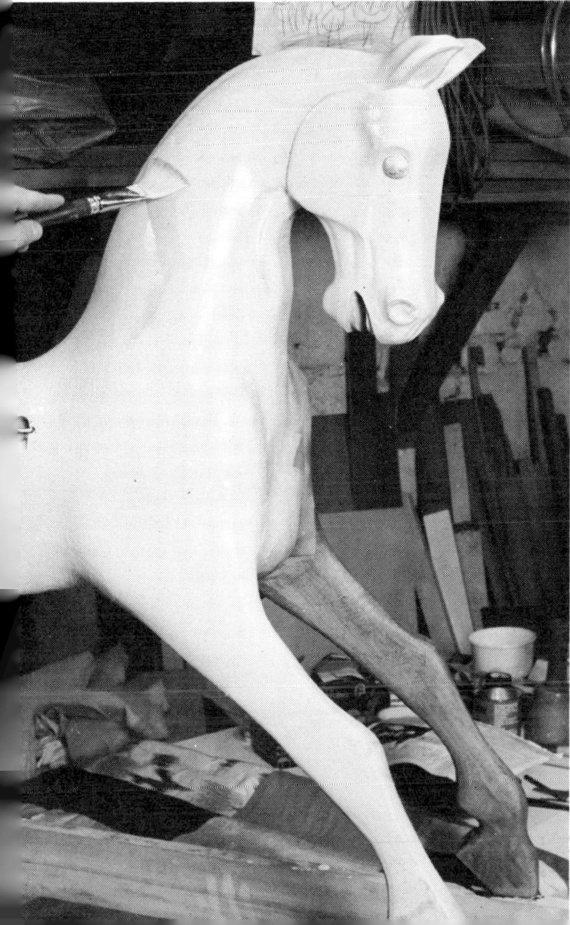
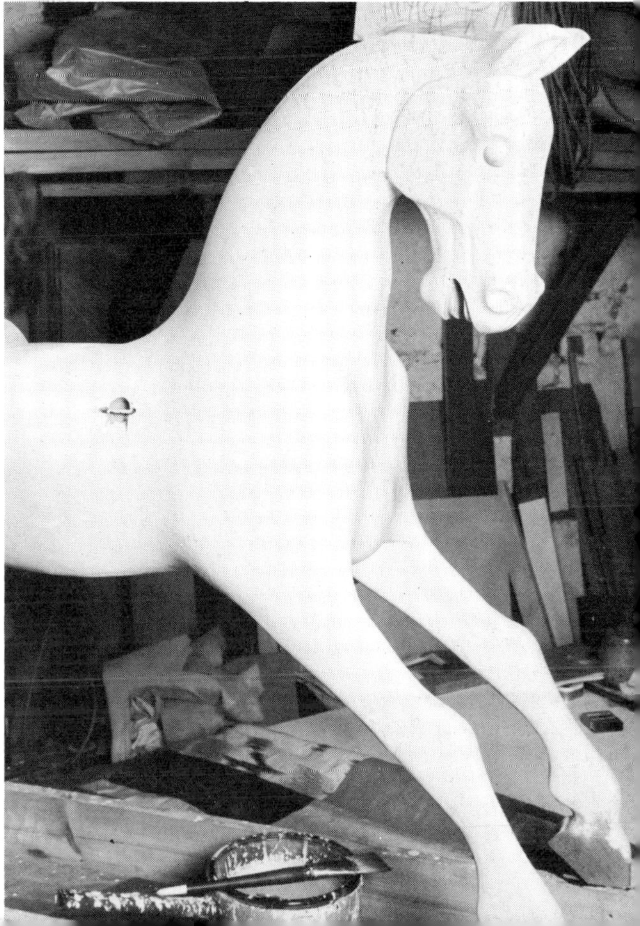

of the brush. After the first coat of size lay scrim (fine-weave cotton plasterer's scrim will do, obtainable from a builders' merchant) along the joins around the body and fix in place with the gesso brush (Plate 109). The succeeding coats will rapidly mask over the scrim. There is no need to allow much time between the coats, and at least four and up to seven or eight coats will be required. Work steadily round the horse, and by the time you get back to where you started you can carry straight on with the next coat (Plate 110). Alternate the direction of the brush strokes, first up and down, then from side to side with the next coat. Watch out for air bubbles and smooth them over by rubbing lightly with your finger.

After gessoing, the horse should be left for several days to thoroughly dry out, when it can be sanded down with fine sandpaper (Plate 111). Before painting it is customary to brush on a coat of shellac varnish to seal the surface.

APPENDIX 3

Rocking-horse accessories and fittings suitable for the rocking-horses described in this book, and for renovations, are available from the author. These include swing irons, swing iron brackets, horsehair manes and tails, glass eyes, brass 'bowler hats', brass dome and fancy nails, dappling pads, rosettes, leather bridles and saddlery, stirrup irons, gesso materials and full size paper patterns.

For full details send a stamped self addressed envelope (or international reply coupon) to:

Anthony Dew, The Rocking Horseman
The Rocking-horse Shop
Old Road
Holme upon Spalding Moor
York YO4 4AB
Yorkshire
England

GLOSSARY

Bevel (a) formed by planing off a piece of wood to an appropriate angle.

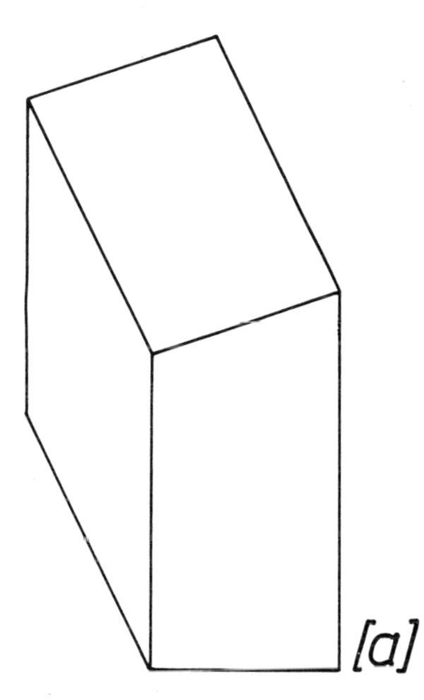

Chamfer (c) formed when a corner of the wood is planed off (usually at 45°).

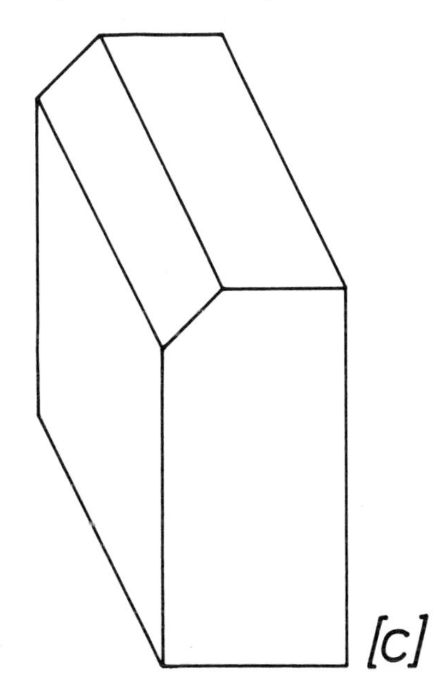

Butt joint (b) where two pieces of wood overlap and are joined together by gluing. It is important that the two faces should make contact over the whole area to be glued.

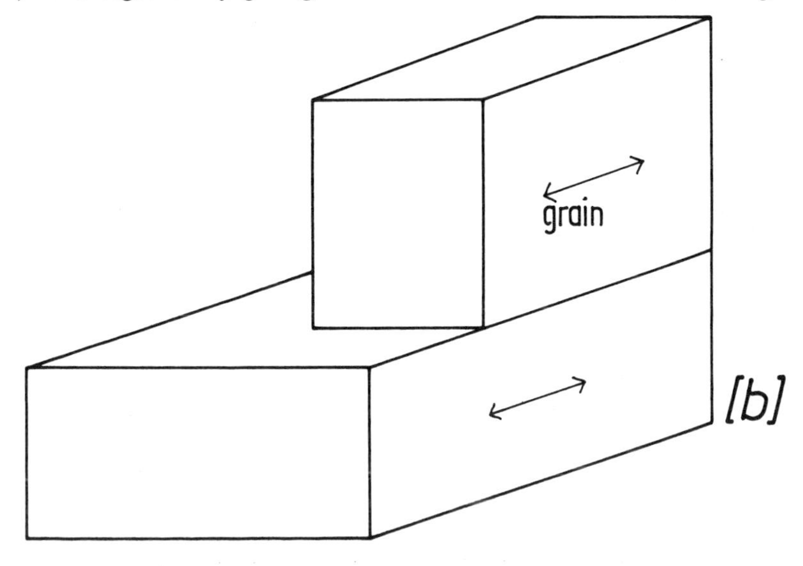

Countersink bit (d) is used to widen out the top of a screw hole so that a countersunk screw head will sit just below the surface of the wood.

Drill bits The twist drill (e) is used for smaller holes. Designed primarily for drilling into metal, it will work quite satisfactorily in wood, particularly if the tip is ground to form small 'spurs' as shown, rather than the standard V shaped point. Used either in a hand drill or electric drill.

The twist bit (f) is used in a hand brace and is normally used for larger holes. The Jennings pattern has a double spiral which clears wood shavings efficiently from the hole.

Flat bits (g) are for use in electric drills. They are simple and efficient but care must be taken if the larger sizes are used since these tend to 'grab' at the wood.

The forstner bit (h) cuts a clean, flat-bottomed hole and is available either with a square shank for use in a hand brace or round shank for use in a power drill.

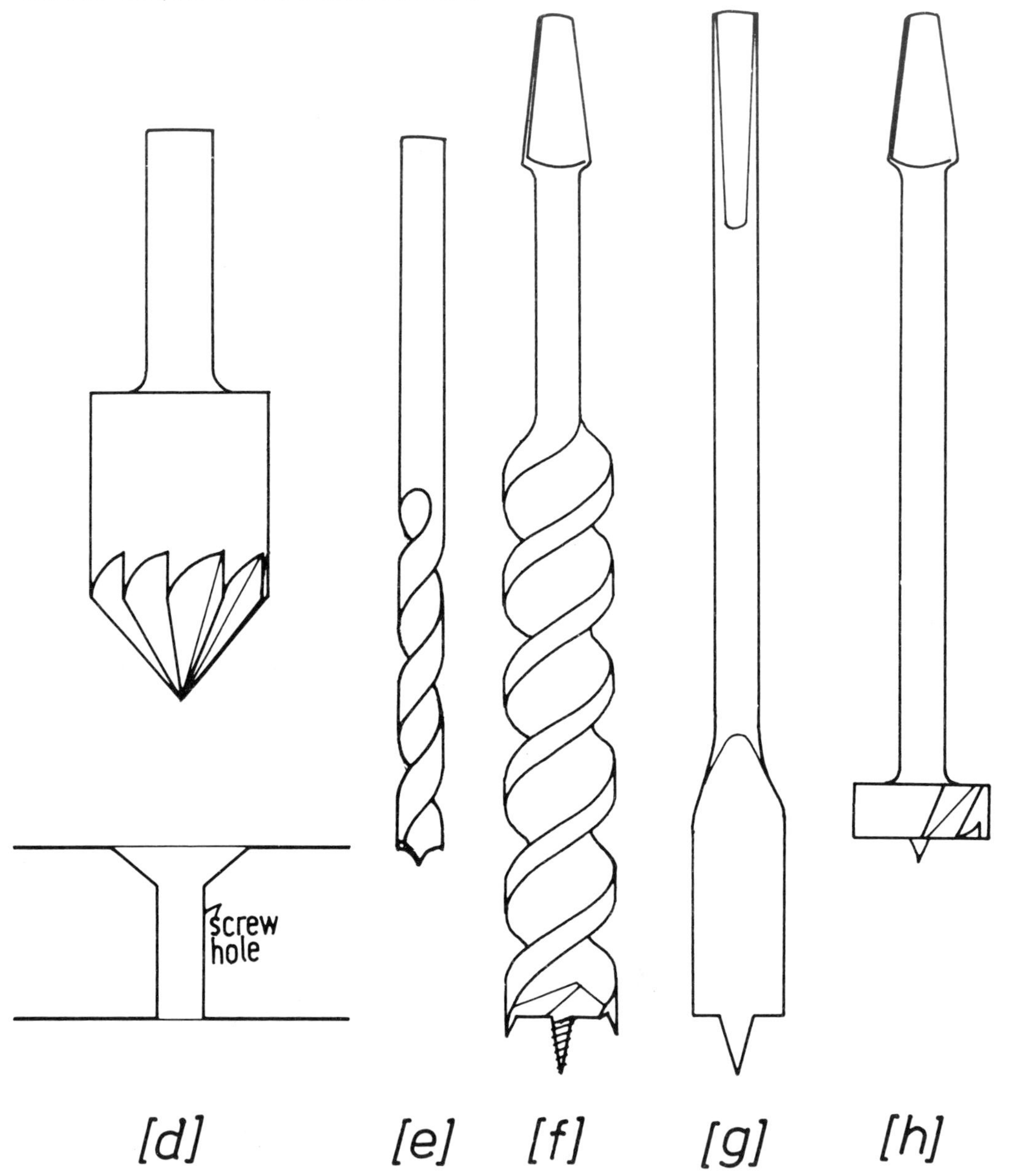

Mortice and tenon joint The mortice (i) and tenon (j) joint is used to join two pieces of wood to form a T shape.

The type shown is that used when making the large rocking-horse stand with square or rectangular posts. The tenon should be wedged in place (as well as glued), the wedges driven into saw cuts made at right angles to the direction of grain of the wood surrounding the mortice.

Saber saw or jigsaw Hand-held electric saw used for making straight or curved cuts. The blade oscillates up and down rapidly.

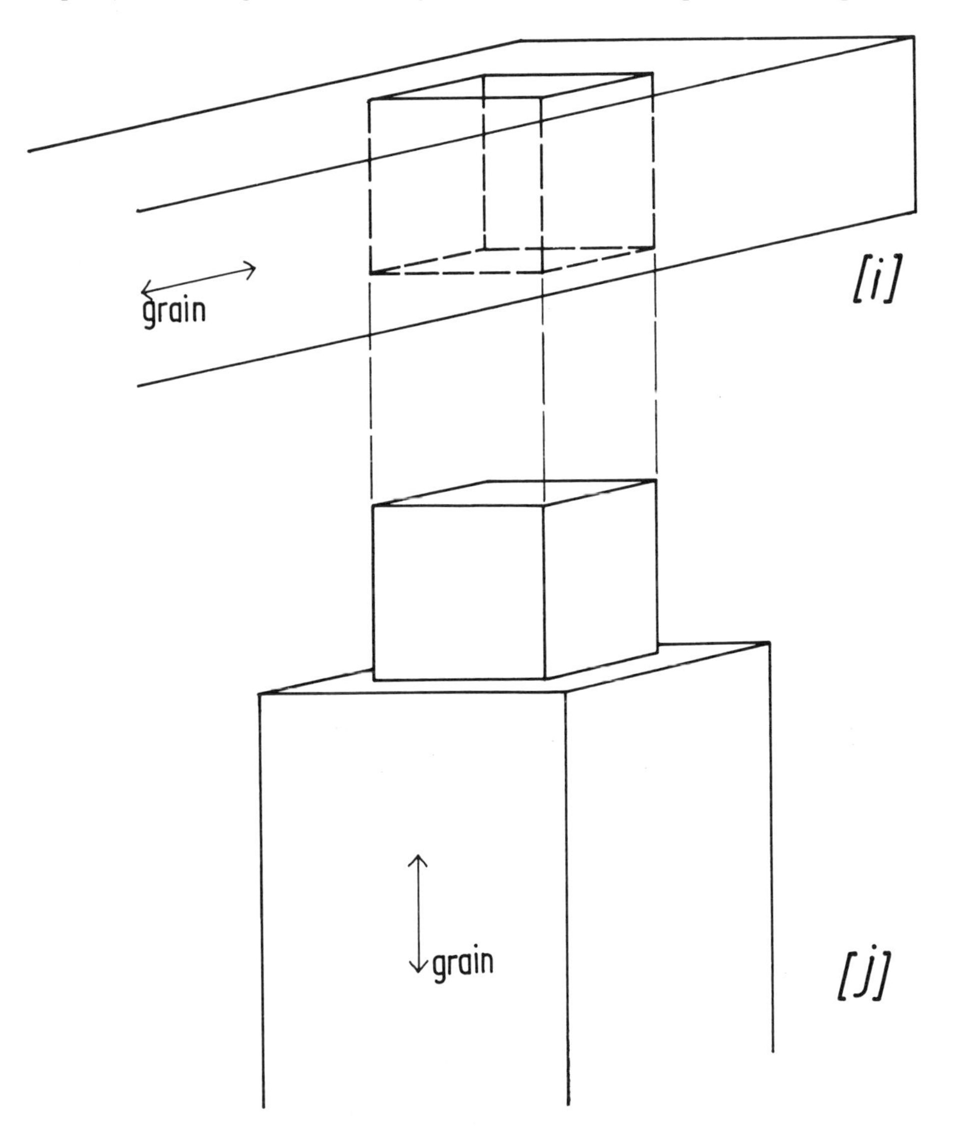

ACKNOWLEDGEMENTS

I would like to thank all the people who helped me in making this book, in particular:

Dr Allan Robson for his generous loans of photographic equipment, advice, and for Plates 1, 11, 37, 69 and 101.

Brian Thompson for his excellent work on polishing the drawings.

Barbara Johnson for so competently typing the manuscript.